Random House • New York

The Block

photos and text by Herb Goro

■ Acknowledgments

I have been very fortunate while doing this book to have received the assistance both of local government officials and of the people whose lives I have been investigating. Commissioner Howard R. Leary of the Police Department, Commissioner Robert O. Lowery of the Fire Department, Bronx District Superintendent #25 of the Department of Sanitation, and the principal of the school on "the block" made it possible for me to interview the members of their departments. Among the residents of the block I would like to give my special thanks to Geneva Smith, John Smith and Suwon Jones for their extraordinary frankness and cooperation.

I have also received much help in assembling and organizing *The Block*. I would like to thank Kathy Flugelman for her excellent assistance in editing, Barbara Gray for her research, and my typists, Hope Tinger and Sonia Tory, who had a very difficult task in transcribing the varied accents of the people interviewed on tape. I would also like to thank Cordelia Jason, my copy editor at Random House, for her unusual dedication.

Finally, I am indebted to Theodore Kheel and the American Foundation on Automation and Employment for their backing, to Lewis Kaden for his general assistance and support, and to Jason Epstein, my editor, whose advice, enthusiasm and encouragement have been very important to me.

HN
80
.N5
G6

First Edition
Copyright © 1970 by Herb Goro
All rights reserved under International and Pan-American Copyright Conventions. Published in the United States by Random House, Inc., New York, and simultaneously in Canada by Random House of Canada Limited, Toronto.
Library of Congress Catalog Card Number: 70-102300
Manufactured in the United States of America

Book designed by Joseph del Gaudio

 110

Manufactured by American Book-Stratford Press

This book is sponsored by the American Foundation on Automation and Employment, Inc., a labor-management foundation that seeks to promote automation by coping with the human problems it creates.

■ Contents

62296

■ Dedication

This book is gratefully dedicated to Clay Felker, editor of *New York Magazine*, whose door has always been open to unknown beginners, and who gave many, myself among them, their first opportunities.

And to the people of "the block" who so generously gave of their time and trust.

■ Preface

The relationship between the American Foundation on Automation and Employment and this photographic essay began when Herb Goro became interested in doing a study of workers displaced by automation. I knew that Herb was a photographer whose skill with a lens was comparable to the most talented writer's skill with a pen. But I was not sure at our first meeting that the human drama which results from the interaction of people and technology could be isolated by the camera. Statistics and sociological analysis do not make interesting photographs. The complexity of the relationship between jobs and technological change is great. A factory which introduces a computer might actually hire more employees, while another, unable to afford expensive capital investment, is forced to close and put its employees on the street.

After talking with Herb Goro, I felt that his own sensitivity to the human condition was captured in the photographs he showed me. His interest in exploring the lives of particular people in a technological age convinced me that there might be a natural alliance between our foundation and this project, and we became a sponsor of this book. It has proved a rewarding relationship, and the product of Herb Goro's sensitive talent is a portrait of life for some New Yorkers that suggests to us how far we all have to go to create a decent world. It makes clear the magnitude of the job to be done if we are to bring all the people into full participation in the society.

The American Foundation on Automation and Employment which I now head was created by labor and management in 1962 to help ease the problems workers faced as the result of automation. At that time in this nation's history unemployment had soared to more than 6 percent of the work force. But even this alarmingly high rate failed to indicate how serious the problem was. The general rate hid the extraordinarily high figures that existed in some areas while there were labor shortages in others. We learned that the rate of joblessness among blacks was generally twice that among whites. For black teenagers unemployment ran at four times the average rate, and for black female youngsters the figure doubled once again.

At the time, in 1962, the country was properly alarmed. A villain was needed to explain why the economy had failed to provide work for all those able to take jobs, and automation was a likely target. The president of the AFL-CIO, George Meany, called automation a "curse." Others came to the defense of technological advance. As too often happens, the battle was joined with a slogan and a catchword. Important issues, which are inevitably complex, were lost. One group of experts called for fiscal measures to stimulate the economy in order to create new jobs. Others looked to remedies for structural unemployment and argued the need to deal with each group among the jobless in specific ways. Both approaches had merit—neither was a complete solution.

The country embarked on a course of economic adjustment, including a reduction in taxes enacted in 1964, to spur consumer purchasing power and thereby reduce unemployment. The rate of joblessness dropped sharply. Indeed, in the mid 1960's shortages of labor began to appear and wages and prices started to rise. By 1969 inflation soon became epi-

ix

demic, and the new aim of federal policy was to curb the economy without making it recede, which stabilized prices without drastically decreasing employment levels.

Through this period of adjustment in the 1960's, one essential fact became increasingly evident. Our affluent society helped those who needed help the least. Persons with skills and education and experience could keep pace with the new technology. Those who were untrained, uneducated and unskilled were left behind. Because many of those who are least prepared to compete in a technological economy are black, the lack of a job exacerbated the sense of exclusion from full participation in the society, and aggravated the divisions between races in the United States.

It is ironic that at this time jobs were available. The development of new industries and a startling demand for white-collar and professional workers had created serious labor shortages in many areas. Employers sought job applicants, and their search was unrewarded. But they were not looking for everyone. They needed persons with the right skills to match the existing jobs.

The answer seemed obvious: job training. But it was not such a simple matter. Job training must be for jobs that exist. The person must be able to get to the job cheaply before he can take it. The training must be for a job that pays a decent wage, one that offers dignity and opportunity for advancement. People have to find out where to get training; they must be able to get the time and money to stay with the training course, and they want a method of evaluating whether they are benefiting from the training.

By now training programs have been initiated by the federal government, state and local governments, companies, unions and community groups in every section of the country. It is too early to evaluate the results.

But in the course of the 1960's we came to understand more about what it means to be excluded from society. We saw what it does to a person to be without a job, without anything to do. We have learned what it means to live in overcrowded and dilapidated housing, to go to schools that don't teach, to play in parks that are resident headquarters for dope pushers, to grow up in neighborhoods that bear no resemblance to the technological wonders exhibited on the television screen. The problem of jobs and all these other problems are interconnected. That might, by now, be a truism—but it is an important truth as well. We know that no one area can be singled out for solution with any hope that it will be the key to the others. But we should realize too that our common goal must be full participation for everyone, that the best solution to the terrible problems of race and poverty in this country is to find the means to offer everyone a role—a good job that provides dignity and security and a chance to move up the ladder. And the path to putting people to work starts with a relevant educational system, training programs that are effective, and government services that work for all sections of the city.

These are the themes Herb Goro went to the East Bronx to explore. From 1968 to 1969 he lived with the people he photographed. He learned their problems. Many turned to him for help. He talked with them and listened to them, and the record of these conversations indicates that as they became friends the tape recorder was not an intruder, nor an obstacle to candor. The stories of the people

Goro lived with are reported here exactly as they were told to him, edited only for minor aids to reading. The result is a perceptive and poignant portrait of urban life among the very poor.

This book shows us very clearly and dramatically the extent of the problem—the difficulty of providing municipal services and economic opportunity to all the people in a way that creates a sense of pride in community and a sense that civil servants are part of a common effort rather than a common enemy; the problems faced by young, black, urban Americans in finding their way through a complicated technological age; the problem of finding the pride and dignity and privacy which are indispensable elements of life. These issues are portrayed with a candor that is rare. Herb Goro's pictures and the tapes of his conversations with these people are free of the romanticism that pervades too much of our discussion of contemporary problems. The people whose stories are told here face seemingly insurmountable obstacles in joining society. Their plight is an indictment of the rest of us, an indication that our institutions and our leaders have not responded adequately to remedy injustice and bring opportunity to all the people.

But this book makes clear also that the situation is not hopeless. John Smith has talents that could be developed. He has pride that should be nurtured. He has ambitions which could be given a chance. Suwon Jones has an understanding of the world that seems to surpass that of many of her more educated and advantaged neighbors. She has a vision of the kind of life she would like. She has a keen perception of her own condition. The others who tell their stories, including the teachers and the social workers, the policemen, the Sanitation men, do not reveal any simplistic or facile solutions to the problem. There will always be tensions in a society as diverse as ours. There will always be strains in building a community. But our tradition and our heritage teaches that this very diversity is the source of our strength. It is our hope that this book indicates the depths of the problem and the challenge to solve it. For in the end the aim of our foundation —the aim of all of us as individuals—is to find a way to build a better community in which all can participate and prosper.

Theodore W. Kheel

■ The Block Worker

I'm a senior block worker here for a neighborhood community corporation. In this community as such, there is no community. I mean that the people . . . it seems to be just a stopping point . . . it's just a point where they stop over and just find a place to live—for a temporary type of period.

The people come here from the Deep South, and from other places—Puerto Rico—and they stop here and they accept these fantastically exorbitant rents to landlords. They accept bad living standards. They accept health problems and things like this. This is true, but the reason for this is because they have no choice. A ghetto has a cycle. A slum has a cycle. It's here one day and gone the next. When I say this, I mean you find there's certain areas in the Bronx that at one time were lily-white middle-income areas. Now the epitome of a slum. It just shows you the evolution. Where I work on Washington Avenue, at one time, twenty years ago, it was a beautiful neighborhood. Now it's a slum. The conditions here are terrible.

You have money-grabbing landlords that refuse to keep any kind of maintenance on the buildings. You have a tenant that's uneducated as far as their rights as a tenant are concerned. You have people that are wards of the state, that are on welfare, and pay these rents 'cause rent money is not coming from their pockets. It's like a whole vicious cycle that goes on here.

You've heard the expression many times—"trapped in the ghetto." This is quite true. You find that people come here, see an apartment, and expect to pay a certain amount of rent for this apartment. What happens is, the person enters the apartment, begins living there. Once he begins living there, he finds many existing problems, like rats and mice, and leaks, ceilings falling in, leaky faucets, the whole thing. And the total expense is on the tenant. In a slum building there is hardly any overhead. A landlord only makes a repair. The only way a landlord will make a repair is if the tenant refuses to stay in that apartment or refuses to pay his rent. And that is the only time a landlord will make a repair.

The Puerto Rican person who comes from Puerto Rico is basically not aware of what substandard housing is. He is not aware that he's being exploited by the landlord. And this goes for a black person migrating here from the South. It's basically the same thing. They're not really sure that they're being exploited and used in a really vicious manner.

I think that the housing problem is like where the kid grows up with rats jumping all over his bed, waking up in the middle of the night and something's crawling on his foot; lifts the covers up, man, and there it is—a ten- or twelve-inch rat, and don't tell me it doesn't happen. I know people that became so accustomed to things of this nature that you ask them, "Do you have rats or mice in your house?" and they answer like, "Yeah. Only one comes in my bedroom at night." Like nothing's happening. Only one. So like, you know, for yourself, for one rat to come in my house would be for me to pack my things and leave. But for these people, they became so exposed and so, like I say, people on the whole adapt.

The Sanitation Department is sort of like an organization that is not particularly interested in what the ghetto looks like. These men feel that they do their

job. They do enough by just picking up the garbage in these communities. They just don't feel that these garbage-filled lots are their problem. Because we have reported these conditions to the Sanitation Department, and they have done nothing about it, and we've tried to get a few people behind us to do something about it. We've requested more pickups per day, but they claim to be short-handed on men and equipment.

Like I told you, it's no community thing here. People are just stopping over. For some reason, people in this community will move from one building on one block into another building on another block, and it's just as bad.

You see, this breaks the community spirit. We get certain people together on a certain block, and they are together as a community and as a group, projecting the same idealism, you know, and wanting the same things done. Now people move in and out of this block, and there's a turnover, and when you go back six months later there's different people living in the same apartment. Just like that, and this breaks the community thing.

Also, you have a problem with the garbage in the lot, because the garbage in the lot breeds health problems—and health problems in a large perspective—breeds rats, mice, roaches, and it also breeds other types of health problems, wherein you can never get any fresh air or this sort of thing. It's sort of like the decaying stink of garbage that lies decaying in this lot. And these fumes constantly seep in through your window, you know, in the summertime in 90-degree weather. It's just constantly decaying, night and day. You're going to get sick.

Like I said to you, these are people that have migrated and immigrated from

Puerto Rico and the South, and they are not aware that you just can't throw a bag of garbage out of the window. In some instances the people just don't care. In some instances they give the garbage to the kid, and he throws it out the hallway window, and he sits there for about fifteen, twenty minutes, and he comes back upstairs with an empty pail, and his mother doesn't know the difference. This kid probably has seen an old wino in the building doing the same thing, so he figures why shouldn't he do it. And this type of thing, this is what a young kid in the ghetto is exposed to.

The cycle of a slum is an amazing thing. It never stands still. In the Bronx the slums move a little quicker than in Manhattan, because in Manhattan you have a community spirit, as I said, and in Brooklyn and in all the other boroughs you have some sort of community spirit going on and inspiration that people stick together. But in the Bronx, the slum will be here on 174th Street in 1975 and in 1985 it will be on 184th Street; and down on 174th Street it may just be through with—you know, just everything condemned—or it may be a rehabilitation process, whereby they'll be moving these very same white people back into this community, and once more the cycle starts over. It's a vicious cycle.

The only thing that I can say that will benefit black people and Puerto Rican people is that there should be a quota and ratio system in the housing, wherein they will have a certain percentage of whites and a certain percent of blacks, which will help curtail this type of thing.

The Block

■ Introduction

This book is about the people living or
working on one block in the East Bronx.
The Bronx has undergone a great trans-
formation since the end of World War II.
Since that time there has been an exodus
of middle- and lower-middle-income white
families, and in their place have come
thousands of Negro and Puerto Rican
families. The Bronx is the only section of
New York City situated on the United
States mainland. It lies north of Manhattan Island and south of suburban Westchester. It occupies an area of 53.1
square miles. The Bronx is one of the
most heavily populated areas in the
nation, with about 33,000 inhabitants
per square mile. About one-fifth of all
Bronx families have annual incomes
below the poverty level, as measured
by the index developed by the Social
Security Administration.

The block I have chosen is within
fifty-five square blocks designated as
one of the city's worst health areas. Its
population is approximately 50,000, with
48 percent Negro, 48 percent Puerto Rican
and 4 percent elderly white. This section
has a significantly high infant mortality
rate (29 deaths per 1,000), a tuberculosis
rate three times higher than the city
average, and a significantly high venereal
disease rate. As a high crime area it
ranks among the worst in New York City.

I would like to thank the people of this
neighborhood, who cooperated with me
to an extraordinary degree. Everyone I
interviewed has been given a voice in
The Block.

Herb Goro

■ The Landlord

I'm the landlord, but that's not my lot. That's a city lot. Just as if it would be my lot or your lot, it would be our responsibility to clean it, right? Well, that's the same way it has to be for the city. And in the same token they should put around a watch that they don't throw no garbage in there. Understand? But the way things are today, they don't care. I see them, the guys from the garbage, throwing stuff there.

The garbage in the lot, actually the city should clean it. At least once or twice a year. Or they should try to prevent that nobody throw no garbage in there. They could put a fence there, maybe six or seven feet high with blocks. And they can give a summons to the people living near to it. That's the only way. If they don't do those things like that the lot is always going to be filled with garbage because the people next to, they're going to feel, Well, why should I go downstairs and bring the garbage? I'm going to dump it down here!

Well, they just feel that it's easy that way. Throwing it out the window. Well, if the city turned around and said, Well, it costs you! Every time you going to throw out garbage it costs you so much.

Otherwise they could turn around and fill the lot up with sand and make maybe something for the kids to play in. Make a sort of playground. Even if they don't put nothing in there—but at least the kids could play and it would be easy to clean it. Right after they had the strike they were supposed to clean it but they just pushed it right inside there because it was raining. Then they said they would come back later and they never have come back yet.

■ The Super's Wife

My husband is the super. I have my apartment free, electricity and a chance for my husband to do outside work. He works in a factory and I help take care of the building. Saturdays and Sundays he cleans. I just clean the building. We don't have to fix anything. The landlord has another man for that. My job is just to keep the building clean.

I don't clean the lot though, only sometimes. I do it because I want to see the building clean, all around the building. Sometimes my husband pushes the garbage in the lot to the middle.

I only have to do the yard and the front of the building and the steps. Sometimes he pushes the garbage because we got the small yard right next to the lot, so sometimes the wind blows down garbage from the lot into my yard, so I clean it up. The people throw the garbage into the lot because they feel tired. All the people don't want to bring the garbage down. They open the window and throw it out. I don't know why. I tell them not to do it because it's no good. There are a lot of garbage cans outside.

If I catch I give a summons but I never caught nobody. I only see garbage. In the night around eleven to eleven thirty I hear it come down. A lot of fires start here and it is rat-infested and the odor is awful.

■ The Sanitation Worker

These people here, they have no pride in their children. Their kids run around half naked while they can go buy wine. They have a filthy neighborhood because after we clean it who puts the dirt on the street, in the lots, us or them? If they want to go out and work and have the things that we have, the things they're envious of, why don't they go out and work instead of staying home on welfare? They're bigber and stronger than I'll ever be, some of 'em, but yet I don't see them working.

That's the whole neighborhood.

There are more family people here. We get along with all these people here, and talk to them, you know? And like more or less we understand them. We get along. You know, there's no conflict between us. We don't actually have any racial disorder between us. We get along very good. We understand each other, but they have their point of view. They figure in life they want to lay around and do nothing. We figure as workers we want to work. Actually I don't feel like I should go and collect unemployment. I can't. I might have a pride to put up in this world but I can't see the idea of me hanging around and doing nothing, just drinking, and throwing cans and just littering the whole neighborhood. Each one of us has two jobs. For the things that we have today, the material things, the home, the car, the family life, the education, the clothing—we work for this. I work here for eight hours a day. I work some place else for four or five hours a day, five days a week.

Nobody in this world ever gave me nothing except my mother. She gave me life. Nobody gave me nothing. I work for what I get. Show me these people out here today that are working. Show me the work that they do—and education, they discriminate against education. My family were poor when they came to this country. They were immigrants. They weren't born and raised here. They came here. They worked. They sent me to school. They made sure I went to school. They sent me to a Catholic high school where they paid fifteen dollars a month. They didn't buy fifteen dollars worth of wine, fifteen dollars worth of stereo set, fifteen dollars worth of anything else. They sent me to school so that I could take the test to be a garbage man. But they worked. I worked. Nobody gave me nothing. These people here, "Give me this, give me that, I have it coming." If they have all of this coming, when I was a child, didn't I have it coming? I waited for a new suit at Easter. When my brother grew out of it I got it. That was my new suit. Nobody gave me nothing. Used to irritate me something terrible. We had clothes being passed down to us when we were younger from our fathers and brothers, but we saw how they tried not to believe in this welfare. I mean when it's Depression and things like that, it's something else. But to live like this here, I can't see people living like this. I don't care how bad off you are, if you got any pride in the world you will go out there and work. Not so far as themselves, more so for their kids, to bring them up in this world and to have a better education, a better viewpoint in life. We went to school and got educated in order to take a test like this here so you become a Sanitation man; you don't have to be Sanitation—cops, any kind of civil service job in this world.

I just don't understand it. Them letting their kids run around in the street and just disregarding everything they have. I

mean, would you actually live in this kind of condition over here? You wouldn't live in there. You couldn't because why would you bring any kids into this neighborhood? All right. Some people over here, I seen them, they are pretty clean, insofar as some of these here supers. They are good. They are clean, but it makes those clean people look dirty. I tell you the truth, I feel so sorry for these little kids that are brought into this world. What are they brought into this world for? They have nothing to live towards in life, unless they are sent out to be educated—their parents are smart enough and try to go out and work and give them what they could, and get them out. That's the only way I could see to get any place, because there's got to be some kind of change.

Believe me, the political world and the government in this world over here today, it stinks. In plain English, it stinks. It does not worry about the people of the United States. They're only worrying about the people on the other side. The people on the other side ain't going to put no butter or bread on our table when we're down and out, believe me. I mean people in general, in all the other countries, that actually this country, insofar as them, our allies, and all of them, even if they're not our allies, we support them, and then we be discriminated by them, we're being thrown down the drain by them. Give it to the people like us, that live in this country, who want to come to this country, who live in this country as Americans, to enjoy democratic democracy in this world. I can't see that you got to give it to these other countries, when people in the street over here that are walking up and down, some of them, even crippled people, they're more needy than the goddam

people over there that don't give a damn. And if they're having any trouble over there, let them fight their own battles. Let them try to secure themself just like we're trying to secure ourself. They're not even worried about their people, the hell with them. Let us worry about our own people over here, that live here. All right. After we take care of our own home front, then if you got to take care of the other people, the people that want a democratic world and live peacefully in this world because actually it's just like a bunch of animals, these people. They only believe in fighting and taking what they could keep for themselves and, in other words, hold tight on everything and don't worry about nobody else. This is going on this way. There's too much greed in this world. Nobody worries about the next guy. If people were more friendly and get along in life, and we could live with each other. I'm not trying to believe on the basis of Communism. I don't believe in Communism. I'm strictly democrat. I like to be free. I don't believe in anybody telling me what to do. I do what I want to do as a working man. My wife works, my kids work. I believe in work. Nothing comes easy in this world. You've got to work to enjoy something. You can't take it easy, because I can never enjoy something that comes easy. Even if I was a rich man I wouldn't be able to take life easy. I think I'd be a nervous wreck standing around. I would like to work. I don't know if everybody's like me, but as far as I'm concerned, as an individual, I believe in work. My kids are working. I brought them up to work. I brought them up for an education. I'm sending my daughter to college. It's going to cost me money, that's why we're all working and trying to send everybody through college. It's a sacrifice, but we love to eat and I love to have the food on the table, and I love to live clean. I hate to live in dirt.

I try to help around this neighborhood, try to do my best, but you see some of these people just don't understand. You go up and talk to them, and you tell 'em, "You keep the place clean, we'll keep it just as clean as you, and there will be no dirt around." If in the event you find anybody around here that throws something, you should tell 'em. Tell 'em like this, "You going to live in this house? How can you come downstairs from an apartment and smell all that stuff or even breathe it up on the fourth floor." You actually got to live in this dirt. I was speaking to a woman on 172nd Street. She says, "Would you do me a favor, pick up this here?" Well, I says, "Honey, I've been picking up that lot over there in that corner actually almost every day or every other day, and it seems to always get dirty." And there's another individual around the corner, I don't like to mention any names. Him I told to put out more cans. They got to end up giving these people tickets. If they don't have ample cans for the people to put their garbage in, and if that don't help, and they still have it dirty over there, then actually the mayor or somebody in this city should come down here and talk to these people, or somebody that's their own kind should come over and talk to them and let them learn, not only today you clean up, you clean up every day in order to live in a better neighborhood. You cannot live in a good neighborhood if you don't keep it clean. The filth—you could make a rich person's house look filthy if there's garbage all around.

I think I got a wonderful job. There's nothing bad about my job. I don't mind

cleaning up. You can't pinpoint it down to certain people. It's just like everyplace else. There's some people that are very good people, but say some of them are married and they don't have no husband or some of them, they're not married and living with somebody else, it's like that there. But, well, I can pinpoint it down to about 20 percent are clean, you get the other 80 percent that just don't give a damn. So you can't expect these 20 percent of people to live in cleanliness and you got the 80 percent that's always dirtying up. Now, you see these people that like to drink around corners, they could get that can, just walk over to the garbage can and throw it in. That's not hard, to pick up a can if you're finished drinking beer, and put it in the can. It makes it easy for them, makes it easy for us, it makes it easy for the super, and the neighborhood will be clean.

I mean you can't expect anything to be clean if you say, well, the Department of Sanitation is not picking up. Now, we can't afford to actually pick up this neighborhood as we go along, and sweeping and pick up, and sweeping. We will never finish our work. There isn't enough hours in the day to do your job, actually. There isn't enough men on the job and I know that Lindsay ain't going to hire any more men to put any more salary with the burden they have in the city. Well, there's not exactly a shortage of men insofar as the work. But to go back and start to clean up and sweep the floor and then put it in cans and then pick up, it's a lot of work in a neighborhood like this here. Now, you get some other neighborhoods that guys are fortunate they're working in it. It isn't as bad as over here. They sweep a little bit up over there, but we pick up our own sweepings. We sweep around the thing where we could get at it and pick it up but it's every day—constantly garbage on the floor. In a way it discourages you, because you're over there, you clean the place for them, trying to see that they live in a decent place, at least something clean, that they could walk in a house and not have to hold their nose, but they should worry about themself because I feel that to me as an individual, I love to stay clean. I don't even want to eat with my dirty hands. I have to eat lunch with my work clothes on, but when I get out of here I go home and shower up and stay in cleanliness. These people should feel that way.

Maybe they feel the misfortune in life that they were given a raw deal, but I don't think they were, because when the Irish had a raw deal, the Jewish had the raw deal, the Italians had the raw deal, everybody, and furthermore, the people in this world that should have the biggest raw deal are the Indians and they still got a raw deal today. So I shouldn't say that these people should open up their mouth, 'cause they should thank God that they come over in this United States and collect their welfare. Years ago when we had Depression we had to go through hell to try and get a little welfare and we used to go out and work and break our back and we didn't get nothing for nothing. Nothing came easy to us . . . listen, everybody's got to go through life with a heart failure. Even Jesus Christ on a cross went through life that sacrificed His life and everything. That's the way I look at it. Everybody can live better in this world if they learn to live clean and understand each other. It'd be a better world to live in. That's all I have to say.

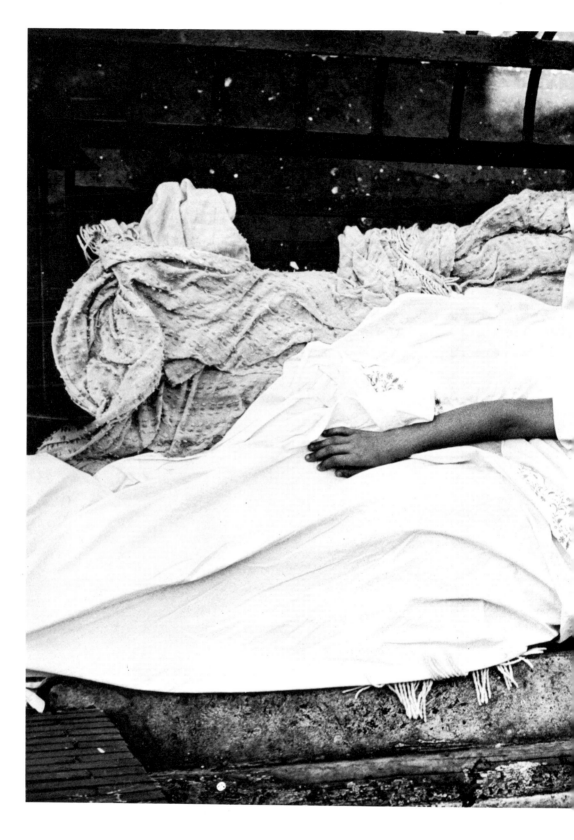

■ The Conductor

I'm just a conductor and I've been work-ing on the Third Avenue El line for ap-proximately three years. I have been working for the T.A. for eight years. The service is lousy. It'll stay lousy, too, if the people don't do something about it. There have been rumors for the past three years to tear down the El. But it hasn't been done yet. There is no proof on it, that they are going to tear it down. There is no hope. You got a lot of people in there. They may be knocking down a lot of areas, but those projects are filled. They got a lot of people there that ride the Third Avenue El. All along the line. The trains are slow. Half the doors don't work. They are dirty, they are filthy. The seats are broken. Everything. In general. Every-body gets after us. We don't have any-thing to do with it. We just operate the doors, open and close the doors. The people come to us. I tell them, "Don't come to me, go downtown. See the man downtown. I don't have anything to do with it." I wish there were better trains and conditions myself. It would be better for me. I don't have to hear from people being cursed out every day. And having things thrown at you.

They throw all kinds of crap. Bulbs, sticks, rocks and everything like that. They are just mostly kids. You know, it's a nice target up there. But this has nothing to do with it. The only thing that has to do with this is when you open the doors on the trains and you jump up on the steps there and the doors are closing by them-selves. And you catch two or three per-sons—you know, you hit them with the doors—and they start cursing at you. You know, "you son of a bitch," and things like that.

It happens because they don't take care of them. The mechanism is so rusted and old and dilapidated that you . . . it just stinks. You tell them this and they try to improvise. Wind it up with rope or tie it up with this or that, you know. Actually they don't have the parts for the trains. They are just improvising. I think these trains are from 1911, and some of them 1939—the World's Fair. On the old trains you can see the date. They got "February something, 1911." That's very old.

We need cleaner trains. The seats are all torn apart. You rip your pants. Woman just about every other day come to me and say, "I ripped my stockings." You know, things like that. They are very dirty, very dirty. Even though they clean them at night. But in general, they're filthy. They clean them, they take out the papers, they sweep them up. They don't wash them down. Sometimes you get three or four doors out of the trains that are not working, and people are running to the other end of the train to get out. We don't realize this, and they get stuck in the trains. That happens plenty of times. Sometimes they don't have signs on them or the kids pull the signs off, and then you don't know.

The people suffer and they bitch to me. They bitch to the motorman and the rest of the guys. They don't bitch where they should bitch. Maybe they don't know how to bitch. Maybe they get one, a couple of smart ones, and they say they're going to write to the T.A. But that's one in every two or three hundred. So you still got the majority that are not involved and don't know anything about it. Mostly what you got is Negroes and Puerto Ricans, you know. I live right in the neighborhood myself. I live in the proj-ects, but I use a car to get to work. The operation of these trains, the conditions on these trains, have gone from bad to worse. They are very bad. The people don't know how to do anything about it. The T.A. is not going to do anything about it. Like anything else. Any department of the city, if you don't keep after them, they are not going to do anything about it. See, when you have an accident around here, you have a few people killed. Like any other place, like when they have accidents on planes. After the accident the investigation comes. The same thing with the trains. Till they have a nice big accident and get a couple of people killed on it, then they'll do something about it.

Now there are a lot of people downtown, the mayor's office and the T.A., that don't know that the Third Avenue El exists. They thought it was knocked down in 1955. I know this personally. You go down to the school here, the T.A. school. They will tell you, "Oh, you don't have to learn about that, you're not going to work on them trains." I mean I got it from new conductors here. I mean it's old stuff, they say. "Don't worry about it, we're going to teach you new stuff." "You never going to work on that stuff." Now this stuff is still here. Now they get up here and they don't know anything about it.

Just about once a day you see kids riding on the backs of them. They hang on the side of the train or the back of the train. They ride it like they were on a trolley. I get them right off. They're going to get hurt or they're going to get you involved. That's what you want to try to avoid, getting involved. You try to avoid these things. But you don't always see them. If you do see them, you're pulling out of a station and you know, what can you do? Pull the emergency cord? Most of the guys around here get them off. The cops ride them off too. We know what the kids are after. They take the bulbs off the trains and throw them down to the people. See, that's their kicks.

Most people here, they are not informed. They get up in the morning to go to work and that's it, they come back. Nobody cares about anybody else. Like if you get somebody after them. You know, somebody who's interested in going around and saying, "Let's get better service here." Maybe if he gets himself a petition and goes around to the buildings here and talks to the people, I'm sure they all will sign it. I got a lot of friends that are schoolteachers here and they complain to me. I say, "You should know better than complaining to me." What can I do, you know. There is a lack of communication. They are not interested. Unless you get after them. You have to push them.

There is no violence on these trains, but you get kids here, you may get a few rocks thrown at you, you know. Stealing of bulbs, just to throw them down and blow them up. That's about all. You get a little violent fights and things like that. But very little of it. Maybe it's because it's such a short ride. Just twenty-one minutes going down, to 149th Street.

■ The Policeman

I'd say it's much tougher to be a police-man today than ever before. It's much harder because you can walk down the street or ride down the street and feel the hatred in the air. You can actually feel it. I treat the people the same way that I've treated them for twenty-one years; but the people have changed. It's not just a real small minority that commits crime today in this area. The vast majority of people do. They may not participate in the actual theft, but two nights ago there was a typical example.

You had seven grownups standing out-side of Woolworth's while two or three kids broke into it. Now, I passed with the radio car. Nobody put up a hand to stop us. Nobody called us.

Adults can stand within ten feet of a telephone, they won't call us. They see a crime being perpetrated right in front of them and they won't call us. They let it go on. They let the burglary take place. It's an accepted thing. Crime is accepted. In certain sections around here we have adults who stand out on the street on a summer's night, let their children break into a store, knowing they're definitely not going to be punished. It's incredible to see.

I brought a boy home for breaking into a truck right over here. I brought him home to his stepfather, and in front of the child the father said, "So what's the big deal, all kids steal." Now what chance in hell does this kid stand? This is what he's taught by his stepfather. "All kids steal." This kid is dead before he lives.

If I answered four jobs in a night—fifteen or twenty years ago—if I answered four jobs in a night I had a fairly active night. If I handle fifteen jobs in a night now, that's a breeze.

Three nights out of five I haven't eaten—you don't have a chance to eat because you won't leave your partner alone that long. We're not going to take that full hour for a meal if you ride in a radio car in a tough neighborhood or a crime-ridden neighborhood. You're not going to leave your partner alone. What we do is we grab a sandwich, a hamburger, and a container of coffee and you sit in the radio car and many is the time you'll eat that hamburger and swallow it and you'll have half of it in your mouth while you're running up the stairs for the next guy. It's a hard crime area. Mainly assault. Assault on each other, assault on passers-by, assault on shoppers, purse-snatching and homicide here. I imagine there are more stickups in a neighborhood like this than in most others, and I know that there's a terrible influx of weapons in the area in the last four or five years. It's very easy to get a gun today, very easy, be-lieve it. They can't do enough to stop it. There's also a tremendous amount of drugs.

I'd say that from the age of nine, ten, up—they don't know what supervision is. Parental supervision. They're allowed to stay out in that street, and it starts in June and it'll end around September, except the weekends. The weekends they'll still be out there, until three, four and five o'clock in the morning—even in the win-ter—either sniffing glue, smoking pot, and some of them are eleven, some of them are twelve years old. Some of the glue-sniffers around here are anywhere be-tween ten and fourteen. They must sleep in the hallways all night long. I don't think they ever go home to their apart-ment. I'd say that the parent couldn't care less. As long as the kid is out of the house and out of their hair, the parent couldn't

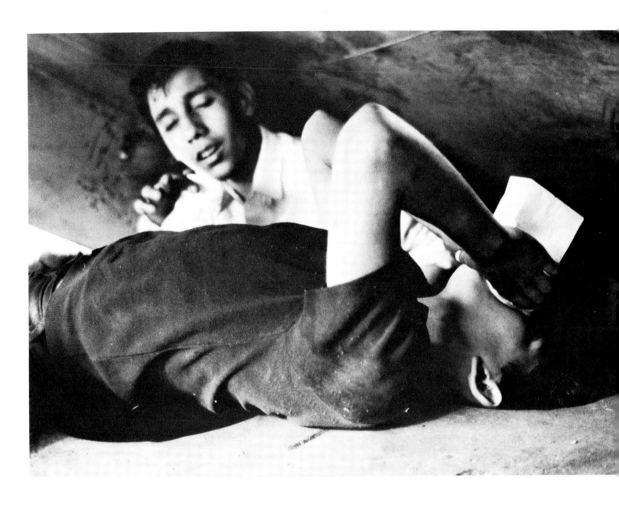

care less. I know kids on this street and probably I care more about them than their father and mother do. Nobody cares about them, and that's why you can't blame the kid. No boy was born bad. No girl was born bad.

I can imagine we can go into dozens and dozens of excuses for them, but I think that this doesn't help the people the crimes are perpetrated against. All the excuses that people think up for crime being committed, it never helps the guy who's laying flat on his back after being struck over the skull with a lead pipe or a small bat. It doesn't help a sixty-seven- or a sixty-nine-year-old woman who has been knocked to the ground and her arm is wrenched, her wrist hurts, we can't go up to her and start saying, Well, this poor fellow didn't have the proper background; this doesn't heal their wound. I think that there's far more sympathetic attention paid to the criminal today than the one the crime is perpetrated against. I'd rather be just as sympathetic to an injured party at the scene of a crime, and possibly a little less sympathetic to the perpetrator of the crime.

I believe in capital punishment. Without a doubt. Without a doubt, I believe in capital punishment. I think that if anyone who were ever personally involved in a homicide—I've been involved in a few, not in my family or anything like that, but in capturing—he'd definitely believe in it. When a man can take a life and be re- leased and come back out and kill again, how do you explain this? How do you explain it to the wife or the children? How do you explain it to these people? When they're hurt time and time again by every typical criminal who returns again and again and again to his crime after crime after crime.

They don't have any more room in the jails, and the sentences are lighter and lighter. We could sit in a courtroom with two burglars who in front of us are now planning their next two jobs, one to pay the lawyer and one to pay the bondsman. These guys aren't worrying about being sent up for three to five years or seven and a half or ten. They're worrying if they'll do as much as a year.

And again, how do you explain this to the people, especially when cases are postponed time and time and time again. Here is a great fault in our society today. An honest man has his store broken into. Now, he puts maybe sixteen hours a day in his store. Somebody breaks into that store and he's captured. Most of the time he's not captured, let's face it; but you capture this fellow. Then the case will be heard in a court. The lawyer has it postponed once, twice, three times. In order to discourage a complainant, cases will be postponed three, four, five—I've had it happen as many as seven times. Now for a guy who's earning forty dollars a day, who has this case postponed seven times, his family is out two hundred and eighty bucks. It's kind of hard to make up two hundred and eighty bucks once you've lost it—to be a good citizen—and this is why the average good citizen says, "I don't want to be involved." That's their answer. "I don't want to be involved." The complainant, the guy the crime has been perpetrated against, it's costing him his livelihood to be Joe Good Citizen and go to court. He's discouraged in a court- room. He can't keep going back and back and back. Because every time he does, even if he's a poor man, even if he has a poor-paying job and he only loses twenty dollars a day, he loses it five and six times just to convict a guy who com-

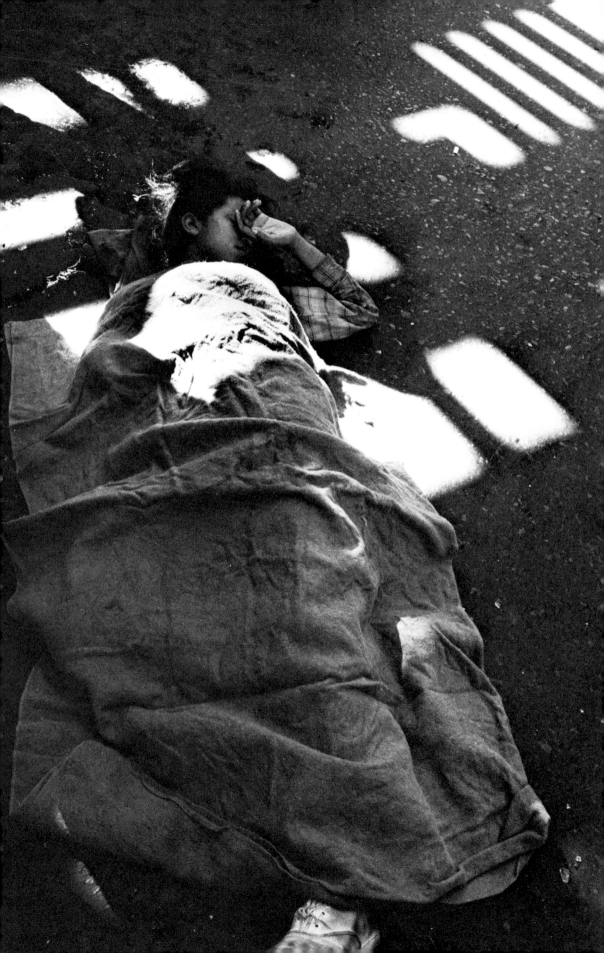

mitted a crime against him. The decent, honest people of this nation are not going to care. They don't care whether the guy gets convicted or not. I had a lady from Schenectady, her car was stripped. I caught the two guys that stripped the car, and the third time she finally came down to New York—three times, and the case was postponed again. She went back to Schenectady and said, "Don't bother calling me, I have no intention of coming down again. Not for four tires." So naturally we had to release the prisoners. We had no complainant. So the next day they're back out stripping another car in the hopes that they get another out-of-towner. In fact if you were smart as a car stripper you'd pick on cars with out-of-town plates in the hopes that their vacation is over.

I have a grandfather who was a policeman. My brother was a policeman. I'm a policeman. My godmother's husband is a policeman. My cousin is a policeman. I've always been proud of being a policeman. I'd say that the finest men that you could possibly meet in your lifetime I've met inside this job. Where else are you going to find guys that are willing to get knocked around as much as some of us get knocked around to help strangers? Policemen can't be as bad as a lot of newspapers and a lot of magazine articles picture them. It turns me over and over, it sickens me to hear us constantly torn apart. When we go out we try to do a job to the best of our ability and it seems that most of the people are against us. I feel a close camaraderie for a fellow cop when he's hurt. It may not hurt me physically but it hurts me mentally when I know that nobody gives a damn about him. Sure it hurts our feelings. And whether they want to believe it or not, we have

feelings. There's nothing different about me than there is about you, and when I'm called filthy, debasing names in the street, I go home, sure, and my hand shakes sometimes. Not in fear, just in plain rage, and I know that the same guy wouldn't talk to me the same way in civilian clothes because I'm six-four and I weigh two hundred and twenty pounds. But I got a number on my hat and another one on my chest and I'm a policeman and I have a responsibility to the community and he knows it and he knows that I'm not going to belt him in the mouth. But if I was in civilian clothes he wouldn't dare talk to me like that because he doesn't know what I'm carrying or whether I'd hit him.

You get out of the radio car and you're perfectly willing to help someone and you're greeted with the expression at the door, "I don't want you, you white motherfucker, I want a black cop." I'd gladly get you a black cop just to avoid your mouth. I'd gladly get you a green cop to avoid your mouth. But if I go to help you, how the hell in the name of any fair treatment to another human being can you greet a man like this that you've never met before. You have nothing against me. I've never done anything to you. I just wore a blue suit with brass buttons and therefore you must hate me?

And I'm not excusing any cop that walks in the door and belts somebody. In fact in twenty-one years and two months I've only known one who ever did things like that and I wouldn't ride in the same radio car with him and I wasn't a friend of his. Eventually he was broken out of his job. He was as sick as the people who hate you for no reason at all. And I don't think he was a prejudiced cop, either. He did it with anybody. It wasn't a question of color or religion. I think the guy would belt his brother if he crossed him. But he was thrown out of his job and no great loss, no great loss to anybody.

I haven't carried my stick in about five years, and even if it's in the car I never take it out of the car with me. When I did carry a stick I think I used it once in about fifteen years. And that was to break into a window. We have had sticks stolen from the car. Naturally you don't have time to lock up a car when somebody is swinging out the window, and if we stopped in the street to lock up the four windows in the car, the four doors, by that time she may have been kicked out the window or fell.

I don't carry a stick in the car. I don't take a stick out with me. Of course this doesn't go for shorter men or lighter men. I'm six-four and I weigh two hundred and twenty pounds. People don't usually fight you directly, no. From a rooftop, yes. They throw things at you. You go up a block, and every now and then you hear a brick or a bottle hit the street alongside of the car. They're aiming at the car. Most of the times they miss.

I'm not worried about it—getting hurt—at all. I have a great deal of faith in God. I think He'll take care of me. I always think as long as I do a job, a good job, where I'm working, I don't think God will let anything happen to me. Maybe that's why they don't have such good aim.

People on the street who before would try to help you or give you information, now no longer talk to you. You're the same guy. They won't talk to you in front of their friends because their friends may be possibly connected with a militant organization or have a particular dislike for policemen and if they were to see their friend talking to a cop, then right away

he's a fink and they have nothing to do with him after that. When a guy says hello to me, well, that's because he's alone on the street. Now if there were four or five of his friends with him he wouldn't say hello.

I don't believe in reaction and I don't believe in militancy. I believe if we're ever going to try to make a decent society out of our whole stupid country—the way it's going now—we're going to, without a doubt, just have to get along. And the sooner everybody knows it the better off we'll all be. That don't mean you have to jump fences to shake hands with a guy. And it don't mean you have to move out of the house if somebody that you didn't like before or whose ethnic background you may have had a poor opinion of moves in.

What I believe in is full equality. Everybody should be treated on a fair basis. It's the only thing I believe in. Well, my grandfather didn't know I was going to be a policeman. He died before I became a policeman. I wish he hadn't. He would have been proud to know that I became a policeman. He would have been very proud. But I don't want my child to become a policeman any longer. We want something better for our children. We don't want them to have to swallow their pride. I don't believe in being a proud man but I do believe that every human being is entitled to some small portion of pride, and when you have to stand by and be called some of the obscenities we're called daily, and to be abused either physically or mentally or verbally the way we're abused today, I don't think . . . I wouldn't want that for my son, no.

◾ The Fireman

The only thing is, I'm a fireman. I'm not a clown out in Coney Island that you throw balls at. Put my head in a hole and throw balls at me. That ain't what I'm getting paid for.

You don't want these people to throw roses at you when you go down the street, but just get out of your goddam way. I mean that's the least they can do. These people, they get in your way. They literally get in your way. You got some guys lay down in front of the rig, right in the middle of the street. What the hell is that? We had a fireman mugged at a fire. Now you don't call this normal. You begin to hate them, and then you become indifferent completely, like a doctor doing an operation. Like he don't know who it is, doesn't care who it is, but he's doing the best job he can.

We sometimes get an applause when we come into it. You get three, four floors going—applause. They're all lined up across the street waiting to watch the show. They have nothing to do. They're selling popcorn.

Well, don't give me any applause or anything like that after the fire's out. That's not what I'm looking for. I get that every second week. We get paid for that. We don't need the applause. But get off our backs, let us do the job. We're not even out at the fire, we're at the box that we're called to, and it's like going to a no man's land. It's like *All Quiet on the Western Front*. Well, for example, I drive

this apparatus. Now, I have to take the shortest and the safest means to get to the box. It's only within the past four or five years that I don't come back the same way any more. I look for an alternate route. They figure you're coming back the same route. They have this thing in quite a few places where they set a booby trap for you. They got this thing set up. They'll point one way and the fire will be the other way, and when you pull into the block now, you get clobbered.

We've had cases where fellows have been really stoned. We had one case in particular. The guy's eye was almost completely put out, coming down from Tremont and Third Avenue, with a rock—but this was a rock the size of an orange. And like the lieutenant, Wilson, he got hit in the eye. This must be going back four years I guess. Pulling the box at four o'clock in the morning, on a wet night like tonight. Nobody in the street, he pulled up, and the whole side of his face is opened up. A big sheet of glass.

This is our job today, protecting ourselves from getting killed with these people—not the fire. The fires we know. We've been taught. You know from experience what you can do at a fire and what you can't do at a fire, but when a human element is involved that's on the other side of the fence, you don't know if you're going to get stabbed, punched or get hit with a milk box—which has happened. One fellow got hit with a milk box. If you just look at the apparatus we're riding in today, everything is covered up. We have places where the men sit with a cover over it, and a door on it, with glass in front of them. The truck companies ride with that little chicken coop in the back. This isn't to help put the fire out, by no means. This is to help the firemen get to

the fire so they can put it out. Now, once he's at the fire, Lord knows what's going to happen to him after that. I mean like he's on the street all by himself. You're liable to come down and find this guy laying in a pool of blood.

These people use the Fire Department as a game, but it's a little rougher game than hide-and-seek when they start off the rooftops. They burn their own buildings with their own families in them. We had a woman here, she was screaming, "There's a fire! There's a fire!" We go running up. They're passing kids out the window on the first-floor level, right? Smoke all over the place. You get around the corner and what had happened I couldn't say—whether it was her boyfriend or her husband or what—but it was some kind of a family thing, an argument. She wouldn't let him in the house, so he poured gasoline or lighter fluid under the door and set it on fire; and she was trapped in there with the kids. Had she been on the third or fourth floor, she'd never have gotten them kids out of there that easy. She passed them out the window to some fellow who was walking by, screaming, breaking windows and all. But they'll do this to their own kind.

And like the other day this lady was sitting out there waiting for her furniture to be picked up or something like that. The kids they put a fire to her bed. That's the truth. I don't know whether they have it in their blood system or not. I don't know what it is but they're doing it. To them it might be a case of, well, it's another activity to pass the hot summer months, or the cold winter months, or whatever they feel.

You see, these people are moving around too much. It's not their community. Nothing here belongs to them, that's what they figure anyway. They don't give a damn whose property it belongs to, I mean they just live in it. The kids don't care whose car they're jumping on. They're given too much.

We do their baby-sitting. We keep them from burning; the cops keep them from killing each other; the garbage men clean up their dirt after them, or whatever dirt they can pick up. Yeah, the whole neighborhood is about the average age of four years old. In mentality and in attitude. And the mayor is their mother and they don't have a father. And you are their baby-sitters for the night. And you can't hit back. You don't hit them and they stamp their feet and they stamp their feet by burning the building. It's the whole bloody city, not these people any more than anybody else. I don't blame these people for anything. I blame these characters who come in telling them what to do, telling them this is your right, telling them you deserve this, this is your money. It's not their money, it's my money. My money is paying for their welfare. You get a hundred dollars taken out of your pay every two weeks, just on taxes, man. Before, it used to buy a mile of the Alabama road—with a hundred dollars. Now they're buying a two-hundred-dollar apartment. They have to abuse me and I have to pay for my own abuse? I'm financing my own misery? That's ridiculous. I'm working my ass off to maintain what some other guy is getting for nothing?

I got six years left. I could probably retire in six years—a fifteen-year job—and I'm getting as far away from this place as I can get, not out of the city, but out of the state, maybe even out of the country. I want to live with normal people—who respect one another, who respect what they got, what you got. There's only two classes in the city—the characters that sit on the top and the characters on the bottom. There's only rich and poor, there's no place for a middle guy—no place. And these politicians are telling you what to do: train them, teach them values. Man, I don't want to live with them; you live with them and teach them. If you wanted to do that, then you should open up Hyannis Port and move in. Five thousand of them. Same with Rockefeller, same with Lindsay.

They don't live with them; they drive through. And when they come in they come in with a bodyguard, about fifty guys. And beautiful, they're going to put twenty million dollars—in this community. Twenty million dollars—the people don't even know how to count that high. And two months later they're still standing there waiting for the twenty million dollars.

■ The Demolition Worker

It takes about one week to tear down a building. Just about a week, it all depends on how many men you get on it. I'd say about 25 percent of the buildings we tear down are in Harlem and stuff like that— all through 120th, 117th, right up all the way up in Harlem. Then we got some on the other side of Manhattan there—154th Street; then through the Bronx, here. I would say they are about equally shared, fifty-fifty. It's a risky business, demolition is a risky business. The pay is very good. As far as the pay, we get about $5.40 an hour, but it's a dangerous job, very dangerous.

If you looked down there in the records and stuff like that down at the union hall, many a wrecker has been killed or hurt, I mean maimed; this is a very tricky business. In fact, it got so it's hard to get a good wrecker nowadays. There is an awful lot of work going on in demolition.

A four-, five-story building, we could take it down in less than a week, that's salvage and all. About 40 or 50 percent of the stuff or more is salvageable. I mean that's all there is to the wrecking business. You have a building, take it down and that's it. Save whatever you can; what you can't save, you destroy.

You know, you can't blame the land-lords, I mean about 80 percent of these buildings you'd be surprised when you get into the buildings there, boy, I'm tell-ing you they're polluted, they stink, I'm telling you. You can't blame the landlord, you cannot, that's impossible, you can't. It's like everything else, if you maintain something, I mean, you will always pre-serve it for the rest of your life. Regardless, I mean, these buildings are up—God Almighty—forty, fifty years and if they took care of these buildings like they should, they'd last another forty, fifty years. It's negligence, it's the people them-selves, that's all it is. I'm telling you. It wouldn't be on the landlord, it would be on the people. You got to be a lazy per-son. As for myself, I moved out from this city. I moved to Long Island. I have a family, I have kids, I have eleven kids. Well, I figured I could raise them out there better than I can in the city. Really, I think it's the people themselves. I realize my job is risky, but the pay is good. It's better than going to a factory—with eleven kids, I could hardly make it. Unless, if you're the type like, well, you don't want to work for eleven kids, I could go to wel-fare and that I've never been on. My wife doesn't work, she does a good day's work with eleven kids.

I happen to be the burner on the job, so just the other day I was burning fire escapes—I burn all the steel and stuff— and I could see some of the people throw-ing water and garbage out of the window. They have about two years of garbage back there. I asked a woman how the garbage got back there and she said, "I don't know but there is two years of garbage back there." I think the people are too lazy to take it down so they throw it out the window. She claims she wasn't doing it, but it was the other people who were doing it. She was looking out the window and she shouted to me, where could she find a nice place to move to. She was asking me where she could find five rooms, so I told her I didn't know because she had a big family, and she said she wanted to get out of this place. When you see the garbage back there, I don't see how a person would want to live around this place. Maybe these peo-ple can't afford to move out, but like

35

myself I was living in Harlem and eventually I was making some money, and I had a family coming, the little ones coming. You figure you got to do better, so we decided to take a chance and buy a home, that's just what I did. We bought a home in Wyandach, Long Island. It's a nice area but it's a long ways out.

The conditions, from what I've seen I can't say it's the landlord. I would say it's the people's fault as well as the landlord. Well, you have some landlords who don't like to fix up, so really that makes it difficult for the people. But then not all landlords are alike. Then you have the landlords that do fix up, but the people tear it up, so I don't know why the landlord would want to invest money any further to fix up. Many landlords are afraid to take a chance because if they invest money in the building they may lose it if the city takes it over. It's a fifty-fifty chance.

There is too much garbage in the street. It's the people themselves, not the landlord. I see it, I know it. They're lazy people. That's a lazy person that doesn't want to have anything. There are some people that I know who are very poor and keep a very clean home and there are some women that I know who have children with no father in the home who go out and work. It all depends on the person themselves. The conditions cannot be blamed all on the landlord. The people know better, but I don't think they care. Between 171st and 174th streets on the right-hand side, them houses, I'd say about fifteen years back, 80 percent of them were Jewish people that lived in them houses and they were immaculate. I mean immaculate. Now, within the last ten years, you go there and see them houses now. They're deteriorating. The windows are all broken, they don't have any curtains, they have rags sticking up in the windows and stuff like that. I never seen nothing like it. I'm not Jewish and I'm not prejudiced either, I'm not. Maybe these people are a different breed of people. So help me. My opinion, I think it's the people themselves, I actually believe it's the people themselves, I really do. You look between these two buildings out here, the lot. Look at the garbage you find here. I blame it on the lack of education of these people, the proper education. They just don't care, they don't give a darn. What they need here is better laws or something. The parents are falling down on their responsibility in helping to keep this community clean and not training their children right. That's what I say. The parents themselves have not been brought up right.

The landlord gets so disgusted, you know what I mean, investing money, money, money. One can't blame them, they'll go broke. So what happens, they can't even pay their taxes. And what happens, the city steps in, they take the property over and they condemn the building. Now, if the city felt that way about it, what they should do is sponsor the program. Go ahead, do what's right. But they don't want to; all they're doing is grabbing real estate. That's all they want. You watch, in ten years from now they'll probably sell it to a private syndicate so they'll make a co-op or stuff like that, and charge these poor fools thirty dollars a room. It's all a gimmick. It's only common sense. Building projects is all they ever do. They force these poor landlords out, because of the heavy taxes. So what the hell, why don't they lend them the money to pay their taxes.

You know something, you can't blame

the people. You can't. You can't blame
the people. What can you expect of them?
They have a dozen kids and they can't
afford to take care of them. I think everything is referred back to the city. It's a
complicated affair. Actually, when I talk
about these problems, we have to consider every little thing. Every little thing.
Like the conditions of living. The conditions of wages. What they earn. What
they don't earn. How much they spend for
different booze, or whatever you want to
call it, liquor. The jobs, education and all
that stuff. In plain words, I say that the
people are ignorant of the fact. I've been
around this racket now for the last twenty
some odd years and I've seen what goes
on. There are some of these people you
have to pity, they don't know any better.
That's why I think these people need an
education. That's the gospel truth. They
should get together, I mean the people
that are well-educated, and try to teach
these people, you know, that don't have
too much happiness and tell them what
to do and how to do it. What's right and
what's wrong. That's what I say. Because,
some of these people, actually, innocently
do things that's going to hurt everybody
else.

You want to know something? Between
you and me, sometimes I'm glad the
people don't take care of the place—that's
why we have plenty of work.

■ The Mothers Speak

When my children are harassed and
made fun of, usually in school, because
of their color, I don't even have to explain
to them any more. Because we have like
what you call the weekly Bible studies.
Just any time that the mood hits me. Sometimes two or three times a week. We have
a Bible study in our home. I'm not what
you call a Baptist, or Protestant or anything like that. Well, to tell you the truth
I'm not anything. Because I'm going to
tell you where it's at. I've tried all these
different things and none of them seem to
agree with me. I've found fault with all
of them, especially the Baptist. I was bap-
tized a Baptist. But I mean there are so
many preachers up there talking about
"do what I say and don't do what I do."
You know, I don't go for that. So what I
did, I started taking studies from the
Jehovah's Witnesses. So I have some of
their books in there and I explain it to
them like, you know, like from the Bible.
When God created the first man he
molded him from the clay of the earth.
And in this man there were all the different colors. You know, like his offspring
came out all different colors. Because he
had all these colors in him. But it wasn't
that way because God meant for anybody
to be better than anybody, but because
different colors make up for a beautiful
assembly. I mean, you know, it's so boring
when everything is all white or everything
it's all black. It just becomes dull. So you
just have a variety of colors. Actually all
this "I'm better than you and you're my
slave," it all started way back in the
Bible since Pharaoh's time. And then it
gradually came to the Romans and the
Spaniards and the Englishmen and now
it's here in America. But, you know, I just

tell them, "In God's eyesight you're just as good as the white man or the yellow man or the purple man for that matter. He made you this color because a conglomeration of colors to God is beautiful. I mean you see a field of flowers, it's beautiful, all these different colors. These different colors make beauty and God meant for the world to be beautiful." So that's the way I explain it to them.

■ The kids play in that lot. You see my kid. He got something in the back of his neck, a rash. I think maybe it was from playing in that garbage down here. The children use that lot as their playground. They play in the lot, and somebody throws garbage from the windows down to the lot where the kids are playing.

Last week a lady from the top floor threw a big empty box, and my kid was playing in the lot and the box hit him right on the head. The city doesn't do anything about cleaning this lot. They don't do nothing. One day the Sanitation men came and all they did was push the garbage back, and a week later it was the same. Every night there is a fire in the lot. Last night, three times. And the kids set fires to the buildings next door, the ones that were abandoned. This happens every night. So I can't sleep. I'm afraid that the building will burn down while I'm sleeping.

■ We have like junkies. Dope addicts. We have winos laying in the streets. There are fights and killings all up and down the street. Right out here on Third Avenue. On this block. In the past year there have been three or four killings on this block. This summer there was a man shot right here on the corner by the subway. There was another man shot down on the other

corner. He was in a car and somebody shot him through the window.

Across the street here, about six months ago, some man shot his wife. And it hasn't been two months since we had our own trouble. Some little kid was out throwing rocks at my windows. So he threw one and it came all the way through and it broke the window. So I told my son Manley to go downstairs to make that boy stop throwing rocks. So Manley went down there, and the kid got into a little fight. So the landlord of this building went across the street and got the child's mother. So she come back over here and she started shaking Manley around and Ellie, my friend, comes running upstairs and tells me that this lady is grabbing Manley's throat and shaking him. And then right behind her comes Sharon, another friend, and she tells me that the lady smacked Manley a couple of times. So my husband David went downstairs to see what it was about. He had grabbed my house shoes and I didn't have anything on my feet. So she started yelling and cursing at him, and she told him about what she would do to him. So David called me downstairs. He told me, "You come on downstairs and talk to her." So I went downstairs and quite naturally I was kind of upset and I pushed her a couple of times, and I smacked her. That would have been the end of it as far as I was concerned. Then she started back across the street and she started calling me, you know, "black nigger," and "MF" and all these kind of stuff. So I went and I grabbed her again. And we started tussling. So her friends come running from across the street and one boy handed her a knife. And she started at me with this knife so I started backing up. And I backed into David, and he handed me a

knife. So I showed her my knife and I said, "Now, you come on." So she threw the knife down and I gave David mine back. And we started fighting again and then somebody else handed her an iron pipe. So when I saw her with the pipe I naturally turned around to run. But when I turned around to run she caught me across the back with the pipe. So, you know, you're kind of stunned. But maybe because I was mad it didn't really hurt. So I turned around and grabbed the pipe away from her and I swung it at her a couple of times—she was running and I missed. But when I swung the third time I caught her. I hit her in the mouth. I knocked her teeth out. She was mad and spitting blood and she picked up another pipe and she hit David across his leg with it. And for about three or four weeks he couldn't even hardly walk on that leg. He had to use a cane. This woman is from across the street. A Spanish woman. When the Negroes say prejudice nobody pays much attention. But you would be surprised at how much prejudice the Spanish people have against the Negroes. And those are the two races that should be the closest together because we are really the underdog.

■ About Rats

Well, we were sleeping and it was two or three o'clock in the morning and I heard a rat scratching on my bed so I woke up my mother. Then the rat runned away over my sister's arm and my sister woke up and started screaming and screaming. Then two or three days passed and my mother was sleeping in the little bed, and a bigger rat than the other climbed up on the bed and tried to get between my mother's legs. My mother shook her leg, and he run away. Yesterday I was watching the TV and I seen a rat—a big, big rat standing next to the refrigerator looking at us.

You couldn't sleep at night. I let my baby sleep with me 'cause we were afraid to let her sleep in the crib. And it got so that like sometimes you would come through here at night and they would run out from under the chairs, and you're screaming all over the place and waking up everybody.

Rats, big rats. I see them. I told Mr. Gonzalez, the landlord. He put poison. But I didn't put it because then the rat dies and smells no good. I can't eat and long time smells no good in my apartment. It smells, smells, smells. I open all the windows.

■ Listen, I've had rats falling in my bathtub. I had to go and buy four big rattraps and I've caught as high as nine big rats. Not mice, rats. Rats that cats would be afraid to tackle. We had to nail down the traps so the rats won't take them away. And they were pulling and pulling, and I found them when they strangled themselves to death. I saved some to show the landlord when he came in. I had the exterminator, but he didn't do nothing. He'd come in and put a little mice feed and spray a little bit and leave.

And every night you hear the rats fighting.

■ Teacher #1

I'm an early-childhood specialist. I have been teaching seventeen years, over seventeen years at this school.

When I started teaching here it was a very difficult situation for me. You had the big problem with those who didn't speak English and didn't understand what you were talking about. Difficulty with the

44

language, that was a handicap. But I found that when they were really bright they would learn. They could come into the kindergarten, not knowing any English, and by the time they left they seemed to learn. I didn't know any Spanish, but I could communicate with them, they just seem to learn despite it all. Now even the Puerto Rican people have become, what shall I say?—Americanized. Language isn't the big problem any more. The problem is with their background—their home life. It's a miracle, just a miracle that some of these children really do as well as they do with all of the problems that they have at home. And, with all their problems they still function. That they are able to get up and come to school and go through a day to me is a miracle when you hear some of these stories.

Well, I guess you have to do something in the home. You have to start in the home. But how far is the function of the teacher in the home? How much could a teacher do in the home?

Well, they say the first five years are the most important years in a child's life, because this is the foundation. These children come to school and they are two and three years behind what we consider the average, and I'll give you some of the examples: they come to school at five, don't know their name, don't know their address, don't know how old they are, don't know the simplest things that most of the middle-income children knew when they came to school. So, already I would say in watching them and watching other children that they are two and three years behind. Now, if you come to school two and three years behind, how can you catch up by the time you are in the sixth grade? I think it is logical that you have to start from the beginning, before they get

into school. If they are in the sixth grade and they are still reading on the first grade level, and you say, "Why?" nobody has the answer.

These people who say that the white teachers are killing, you know, murdering the black—I can't believe that, because I see these teachers working so hard with the children and really, really sincerely wanting to do a job.

They found the challenge here so great . . . I guess you feel in a sense that other children would learn anyway. No matter what you did, they seem to learn, the so-called middle-income children. With these children, though, you have to give them so much more.

Now, what you want to do is make life for them better; the more education they have the easier it will be for them to get a job and make a better life for themselves and make life a little beautiful— they certainly can use some beauty in their lives. You have to feel that you are doing your share . . . you have to feel you have to train these people for jobs, you have to give them this good self-image. You have to give this to the grownups, too, as well as to the children. This is the important thing, to make men feel like men, the women to feel like ladies. This is what is happening today, a social change, and you have to know it. We, as teachers, how far can we go? Now, these are things we haven't done through the years, you know, too much of. What we are trying to do now is really work at it ten times over what we did before, because I think this is it. You have to make the child think he is a little something special and important, I think that is the crux of it, because if the parent is so low down and depressed and can't give it to the child, then we can do part of it anyway. These are the things we are trying to do to help.

When you start to do something new your hope rises again because you feel maybe this will do something for the child. I mean, there is nothing like one-to-one relationship with the child to build up his ego. I'm also in charge of building up the culture study of the minority groups in our school to give the kids a good self-image of themselves. This is very important, so we are trying to do that. Many teachers say, we did it, we had it tough and we did it and why can't they do it . . . but we say there is a difference, there is a certain something that happened all along the way . . . I mean, this is why we're trying to build up the black history, trying to build up the big image: they lost something along the way . . . they had nothing to hold on to.

I find now we are using so many different methods and there are times when you feel that maybe there is either something wrong with you, or . . . you know there is something wrong somewhere because why aren't these children learning the way they should? You are giving so much and most of the teachers do, they really do. Some of them may not be as effective because of their personalities, but I would say in a school like ours 99 percent of the teachers really give their all. So, somewhere along the line, is it the method, is it the child? If you think it is the children, you know, born in a certain way, then you would just want to give up, forget it and go elsewhere. But, if you feel that it has something to do with the way we are handling it, that there is someway that we can help their background, you feel that they can learn.

There is a goal in our school for smaller classes, a smaller teacher-pupil ratio, and we are working towards that goal. We have the nongraded programs so that the child who has the ability, who has the urge and has the desire can move ahead, while the others who are not as bright, or haven't reached this particular level, can go slower and not hold anyone back.

You try this way, you try to get more equipment, more people to help. I try to be optimistic. We are trying many different ways with these programs, these experimental programs. We are trying to get people from the community working in our school. My principal is trying to get more people and a lot of bilingual people who know how to speak the language to make the parents and children feel more comfortable. We are getting a lot of help.

I am a little more flexible than some teachers who feel that because they've done something all the way and it worked for the children in the past, why shouldn't it work for these children. They think this is the way you do it. The children must conform, they have to, this is life, you can't do what you feel like in life, you go to a job. You have to be there on time, you have to look a certain way. You have to get along, and so you must train the children for life. I feel the children are also living each day, so you not only train them for life in the future, you train them to live now. I feel you have to be more flexible, you have to show affection. Some teachers feel that affection is not part of their job. I feel you can't treat every child the same way because every personality is different. Some children react better to a softness, a gentleness. Some don't react that way.

A great teacher is one that the children can relate to. That they can feel that they want to work for and that they want to do almost anything to please the teacher. That the teacher makes them feel important, makes the children feel important. Makes them important enough that they want to learn.

You have to give them an individual touch. You have to notice the child in some way and make sure that that child knows that you care about him.

Of course the ideals are not always what you can do. When I started to teach, I had to just, you know, throw some of my ideals away in the sense that they didn't function, you know, didn't work in this kind of classroom. If you don't get some real conformity, you would fall apart because you have to have them all quiet at the same time, you have to have a certain regimentation in order for me to survive and for the children to survive.

Well, we are trying now. In the olden days, or when we first started, there was one teacher with about forty children. We now have a set up where we have three adults with thirty children, so we are doing more.

That's right. Two adults and a para-professional. The para-professional is the community person who has a high school diploma or an equivalency and is going on to college. We have to have more programs. You have to give them more materials, more people, more of everything in order to compensate—compensatory education—to compensate for their poor home lives. If I didn't think that there could be some compensation in this way, then in some cases it would really be hopeless. I can't see it. I can't see something being hopeless. I think you must always fight for something and in whatever way you can, even if it is in a small way, but there must always be an alternative, or something else that you do. Or if this doesn't

work, let's try this. There must be something. You have to feel somehow that what you are doing is going to help the child. That you are going to reach him. You may give up on one child sometimes and say, well, maybe this is not his time and we will do the best we can with him and maybe next year he will get a spark or maybe we can reach him in another way. That is why we are trying to do things all the time, because we say, well, if that didn't work, let's try something else. Let's try a new method. Let's try some new materials. Let's try a new approach.

The teachers are confused too. Most of the teachers feel, well look, I'm doing a job, I'm working hard with the children. Why aren't they doing better . . . if I'm doing my best. I've worked with other children, you know, the middle-income children, and they learned. Then it must be something wrong with these children. It can't be me . . . so you think, well, it's the home, okay, it's the home, yeah, the teachers say, so then it must be the home . . . right . . . If it's the home, well, what can we do about it, we can't do anything about the home, so it's not our fault, let the parents do something, let the people do something, let them, you know. But maybe even though the teachers are working hard, they are not giving what this particular child needs or the approach is wrong. The only answer I have is, keep trying new things.

Still, I truthfully, honestly feel that the public school can offer a lot. I would send my child to public school. I would unless it were an exceptional child. A child who is oversensitive, or a child is just not conforming. It is hard for a nonconforming child to function in a public school. But if we are talking about the middle-income child who is well-adjusted, he can function. I see the children around me. My friends and my relatives. They are all learning. It is those children who can make it and I have seen it in our school, too, the outstanding children. They make it. They get to the schools that they want to go to. I would send my child to the public school, I might have second thoughts about it . . . say, gee, maybe, will there be problems? Maybe I would not be able to solve these problems. The point is this. If they were all sending their children to the public schools, then you would have your balance. But, if they start to take them out, then you lose the balance. Comparatively speaking, the real problems are really not the majority of the children; I'm not talking about behavior, or the work angle, but about children who will do things like take money that doesn't belong to them, saying "You give me your money or else," or fighting. Really, when you think how many children are in this school, there's a very small minority that do these things, that really do these actions. I feel it is exaggerated. I really do. Maybe the junior high has more of it because that's what people tell me, but I don't always listen to people because they also tend to exaggerate and build up things. I don't mean there isn't a problem in the sense that the children are not reading on their levels. Why must a six- or seven-year-old be on this level? What if they end up reading and they end up liking to read? There are certain jobs where you have to read well, and there are jobs where you just have to read.

The frustrating part to the middle-income people is that a white child and a black child both have the same average and the black child is getting into the college where the white child doesn't. They feel an unfairness about that. I tell them the black child was handicapped all his life, so we have to give him a break and we have to push him ahead. I feel if there are two openings and two people have the same qualifications, the white and the black, I personally feel the black should get the place. Because I feel he has been deprived and he needs that break.

I look at the bright side of things. I try to—if there are two sides to look at, I'll look at the brighter side of things. Even though, I mean, I see the reality of things but . . . well, we're doing the best we can but something, you know, something is wrong because why are we doing the best and—nothing, you know—we're doing the best we can, and why aren't we getting results. Something is wrong. And, yet, on the other hand, we are certainly doing many new things, we have many new innovations that we never had before, all these new people coming into the schools that we never had before . . . I don't believe they're not genetically as smart. I have never believed it. If I believed that, then what would be the use of all the struggle here. Maybe diet has something to do with how they're learning. We can get to talk to the parents, we can help them as far as lunches, we can help them as far as going to clinics. I don't know. We haven't done enough of this yet.

I've always wanted to be a teacher— it seemed like such an important thing to do. It was scary. I guess I was mature enough at the time to realize how scary it was that you could help mold a life— you know. There's nothing else that I would want to do. Nothing else. And my husband asked me about retiring. I have eighteen years. And I said that I have no desire at this point, you know, thinking of retiring. This is what I want to do.

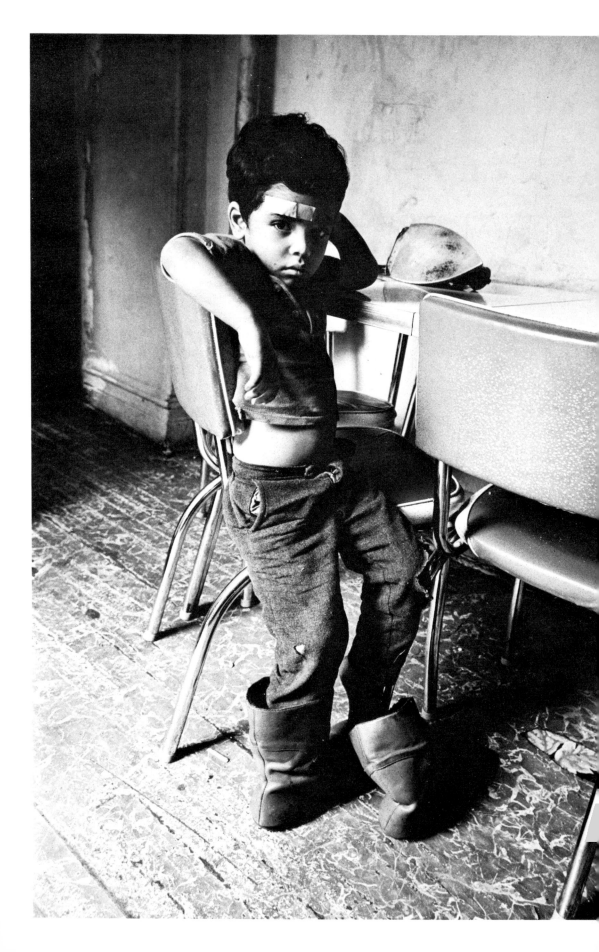

■ Teacher #2

I've been teaching here since 1941. When I started teaching, there was a new theory. Dewey was the God of the educational world with his philosophy of education: education should be for life, and they had a lot of new vocabulary to meet the new ideas. But the important thing was the difference in relationships between supervisors and teachers, and children and teachers, and a greater understanding of the child's background and his home life. And the thing that stands out most in my mind was that there was a troublesome child in my class, one child, whereas today it's hard to find a child that's not troublesome, and that's the biggest difference.

Today, most of the class is almost impossible to manage. And teachers, we always want to put our best foot forward. We don't want anything or anybody to say "Her discipline's bad," because a hangover from the old days is that a teacher is evaluated on the basis of how her children perform. If a teacher goes into the office and says, "This child is impossible, I find it impossible to manage him," they will immediately say, "It's your fault." So when a principal says to a teacher, "How is this child?" she'll never say the truth. She'll always say, "Well, I can manage him." How much blood does a teacher have to spill in order to manage a child? If a child is so difficult that he wears a teacher out he doesn't belong in that classroom. But, no provision has been made for children who are a disturbing influence, because you have politics; you have parents; you have community involvement and you have principals who don't want to go to the superintendent with any complaints.

Principals too are marked on the basis of performance and not complaining. You complain to your immediate supervisor and she may tell the principal. If it gets to the principal, he may tell the superintendent. But probably no one will be told. Believe me, it hardly ever gets to the proper authorities because they're all afraid. So, that makes it very difficult for the teacher and creates all kinds of tensions. And the more things that distract you the more difficult it is for you to control the children.

Let me tell you about a fifth-year problem. They asked me to take the glee club. I was a first-year teacher, but I like a little music and I'm fairly competent when it comes to getting children to doing things. So, I sent around to the teachers and in a very unsophisticated way said, "If you have any children who would be interested in the glee club, send them to me." And the teachers, naturally, took out their problem cases and sent them to me. You can't blame them. They wanted a half-hour of quiet in the room too. So, we had the whole auditorium filled with kids who were not interested in music. One of the little girls was a child I had had in the first year. She was a little frail Puerto Rican child and she wore practically no clothes. The worst storms of the winter she would come with a thin little cotton dress. I found out that she had a sister in the health class. I sent for her, and she came in very fresh, swaggling. I said, "I'd like to see your mother because Norma isn't dressed properly for this weather." The mother came the next day during my lunch hour, screaming and abusive about having to come to school. And she was very nicely dressed. With all her screaming and all her abuse, she sent her child well-dressed the next day.

Suitably dressed, with underwear and sox. That child grew up and used to walk the streets. They used to bring her home three in the morning, while she was still in our school up to the sixth grade. Well, in the glee club one day, I gave an order to the children, and she got up and she let me have it . . . four-letter words. "Go to hell, you so-and-so and so-and-so." I said, "Norma, go out and I don't want to have you here." The next day, the teacher said, "*Please*, take her back. She'll apologize." Well, I wouldn't have any of it. She never came back to the glee club. That's in the fifth and sixth year you have that. A few years ago we had on our faculty a very competent woman, and she was very creative. Her children did the most fabulous things. They put on musicals, and little dramatic selections. Now, I wasn't present, but this is how I got it. A child came up and she said, "Why did you come up the wrong staircase? Go down again." The mother came that afternoon and laced it into her. She let her have it with her fists. Now here's a woman who had been teaching many years. A gray-haired woman who had earned the respect of everybody in that school and the mother didn't care. "She made my daughter go down, up and down." That's all she cared about. That's the kind of thing you have to contend with on the part of the children and on the part of some of the parents.

The mothers don't do the elementary things we expect from a mother. Now, you know no teacher can really substitute for a mother. It's true that she tries to be a mother, the five hours that she has the child, but the child needs more of the genuine motherly affections than a teacher is able to give. The child may love her, but still she goes home to a mother who isn't there, or a mother who is carrying on a little flirtation on the side, or a mother who never gets up in the morning to see that those children go to school. A mother who is busy parading with the militants. I had a woman come in, a nice woman, and I said, "Does your husband work?" She said, "I have no husband." Now, she had three children in our school, three different names. And she didn't say it to me with an air of bravado, neither did she say it with an air that she was doing something wrong. And I certainly wasn't going to criticize her. But, it wasn't good for that girl to be in a household where she had a different uncle every six months. I don't know psychiatrically what it did to her, but I'm sure that it couldn't have been good. It's not a good influence. Well, I also think the genes are very important. That doesn't mean that education should be thrown out the window because let's say we know that a child comes from a bad background. You don't know. You don't know if the child has inherited genes from his father or from his grandfather, or some great-great ancestors. Still, I think the genes are important. Now, let's see why I think they're important. I come from a very large family. There are seven girls and three boys. And, my father came here when he was three years old. My mother, when she was ten. My mother had a little public school education and my father had less because he didn't have shoes or pants and he was the youngest of a large family. In my family you would be surprised in the differences among us ten children. Yet every one of them went to college with varying degrees of success. So I see that the environment is not a total factor in the development of the child.

Some children respond very well to the

53

teacher's efforts to teach them to read. And some children are slow. And they're always slow. Some children will never get beyond the stage of reading the news, a tabloid, a picture newspaper. You know, people vary in ability in every line. Some children take to reading like a sponge to water. They just grasp it. The minute you present a new word they know it. Other children require a great deal of drill, and concentration, and repeated and repeated attack on the new word. Now a bright child really gets along with a minimum of teacher attention, because I've always said, "That child doesn't need me in the room. He's so alert. He brings something to the class. He doesn't wait for me to bring something to the class." Now you take even the non-English-speaking child. You do this, or you motion . . . He responds. A movement with your hands . . . he responds if he has a normal amount of intelligence. Some children just don't move. Now it may be because they're shy; it may be because they're a little immature, but the bright child regardless of his age, he may be five, comes right up to you. You have similar problems in the middle class, but somehow they don't have the intensity that these children's problems have. Of course in the middle class, they don't all have a long span of attention; they're not all articulate. They don't all respond to the teaching. There are many middle-class children who can't read or who are emotionally disturbed or are in some way retarded. But those parents are taking care of their children.

Still, even among white parents, you have people who think that the school is responsible for the child not being able to read; even though the parents may be intelligent, when it comes to their own child they are blind. They refuse to see

certain things, and of course I don't know if it's the place of the school to expose a child to a parent. I don't know how truthful you can be with a parent, because scientifically we have nothing to stand on. We don't know that the child will not do better. It's such a gamble, in anything that we teach him.

Once I had this little boy in the first grade. The mother was the most gorgeous-looking black woman. I wouldn't dare say "black" in those days, but today we call a spade a spade, and they want us to say black for the Negro people. She was gorgeous and I think he was her only child. She had the sweetest personality, but that little boy landed in Warwick—what do they call it? A training school? A reformatory? From there, I think he was in prison. Well, there was something in that child. He didn't respond to any of the good influences. Every teacher tried her hand with him. The mother couldn't do anything with him. He was a problem right from the very first day of school. He was a problem child. He used to stand right in front of my room and beat up, have a fight with another child. And there was nothing I could do about it. Oh, I'm sure the environment plays some part. The child may pick up something and the mother or an adult may say, "You know that's not yours, you cannot take it home." That's environment. He's learning from his environment that some things belong to other people. We learn a lot from our friends. They're so concerned about sex education being taught in the streets. It's not a tragedy to pick it up from your friends. You might learn the wrong thing, but eventually you will learn the right thing. We learn many things from our social intercourse from our friends and people in the streets, from neighbors.

A child who is responsive to learning, learns all the time. Now, if we had smaller classes we could manage a little better. It might give the child that little bit of extra attention, and maybe that would be all he wants. Or you might even talk to a child, and complain to him that he mustn't take the opportunity of other children away; that he'll get his chance, but he must also give the other children a chance. You see, I'm stern. I don't hit the children, but they don't know what I'm going to do, and I have that ring of authority in my voice, so they take notice. Maybe they don't have that ring of authority at their homes.

Now, last year, I had a little boy in my class, a beautiful child, nice, well-built, tall, a Puerto Rican child; and the father came. A very handsome devil, a real no-good. I'd judged him, the first time I met him. I might have been wrong. He came with a woman who was supposed to be the mother, an Irish woman. I never saw her again. The next time he came, he came with a Puerto Rican woman. Now, I used to take the Third Avenue El home and I'd meet this little boy and his sister, who was in the second year, and the father. The little boy and girl ran up and down the platform. The father stood over to the side. I asked, "Where are you going, Robert." He'd say, "My father's going downtown; my mother's coming back; my mother works; then my father'll go to work." Well, he was such a difficult child. So difficult to manage, but there was something so sweet and lovable about him that I overlooked a lot. Now, what did he do? He hit his classmates. On the line, he'd push on the stairs. He did physical acts of violence. You couldn't let him go into the closet to hang up his things when the other children were there, because he

would hurt somebody. The father didn't pay any attention to him. There was no authority. The father was living with this woman, and the woman wouldn't manage the little boy, an ignorant, uneducated woman. His mother ran away and left the little boy and the little girl. One day he was cutting up, talking to children, running around the room, not in his seat, he would never stay in his seat for any length of time. And, of course, I maneuvered to give him all kinds of jobs. Suddenly, there's a deathly silence in the room and everybody's looking at Robert. I turned around, and you know I'm not so young anymore, and I'm not so unsophisticated. But, that child was masturbating. I thought I would die. I ran out of the room and I began to cry.

We're very lucky in the two guidance counselors we have now. The one we had previously used to say, "What do you do that evokes that kind of behavior?" when a teacher complained about a child. Now that's the worst thing you can tell a teacher. You're saying she is a foolish woman and doesn't know how to handle children. Saying that is like holding a red rag before a bull. But these two girls are really very sophisticated and very sympathetic. They assume that the teacher has not caused the child to act that way. And they're right. Because this child's behavior isn't something of the present. This is the kind of behavior that the child's been giving his parents, his neighbors, his friends. From the day he was born he was like that.

They said they would give us smaller classes. Now, last year they started the double session. They had two teachers in the room with thirty children. Each teacher was responsible for fifteen children, and that was the biggest lie that they ever per-

petrated on the parents. You come in the morning and the other teacher went out. Before you could really accomplish anything, she came back and you went down, either to the auditorium or to the yard. If you were in the yard you were in a gym period with either three or four classes. So, there was really very little personal relationship between you and those fifteen. The purpose of having fifteen was so that there would be closer communication between you and the child that needed that little bit of extra help.

It's a fake because the children are not with their official teacher for the whole day, fifteen in a group. Now, when you go out on your preparatory period, your prep period, the other teacher's left with thirty children, instead of fifteen.

And you know, there's another factor I want to tell you: the blacks have been complaining about the school's inferior education. They think if you have more blocks and more puzzles, more games, more . . . games, more toys, it will be a better school. If we could only get across to the parents that these are not the things that make a better school—the things that make a better school are the children who want to learn or who are able to learn. If a child comes to school and has to take another child's snack, something is missing in that child's home that doesn't cost a million dollars; it just costs a little maternal effort and paternal interest. If a child comes to school without any breakfast, or if he's seen things at home he shouldn't see, if he's seen fathers abuse mothers or children, he can't come to school with an open mind and a happy mind ready to learn.

The city is spending millions of dollars on things. The teacher doesn't have time to use all the games she gets. You wouldn't believe the supplies we get. I don't know if the teachers tell you the truth, but I know I haven't got time to use them. These are all recent ideas since we started with all that commotion of the parents wanting to be involved. Now, there is such a thing as parents' interest. We had it years ago when parents were interested. Parents came to a Parents' Meeting in the afternoon. Now, today, they're very conscious that they want their own vocabulary: "Oh, man!" To me it sounds like the language of the gutter. Or they would mispronounce words, and yet you're almost afraid to correct a child to teach him to say ten cents instead of tin cents. Because many of our colored teachers say tin cents. We want the children to speak at least as well as the average person in a big city speaks. I don't mean the uncultured, unschooled person. I mean a person who has had a high school education, or a college education.

We also have the problem of the Puerto Rican parent who doesn't want his child to speak English at home. Because when I say, "Why don't you talk English to the child?" they say to me, "I want her to speak Spanish!" And I tried to tell them that we don't want the child to forget Spanish. It's a sign of culture to speak more than one language, and the child will be a better American citizen if she can speak more than one language. She can bring to our American culture many things from her Spanish ancestry. Maybe we should teach mothers what being a good mother is. I think it would be a good idea to have classes for parents. I don't mean blunt and hurt their feelings, but I think it's very important for the Puerto Rican parents to speak English. I always say to them, "A half hour in the day when you're all sitting around the table, just for one half hour have an English conversation, an English lesson. Say to the child, 'You must ask for whatever you want in English, you want the bread or the meat. Let's all talk English,' and then the rest of the day you can talk Spanish. You'll learn from your child and your child will learn from you." I think that everybody should retain the characteristics of what their forefathers gave them. I think it enhances the culture, it makes for better understanding among different people.

I think you can have an integrated society, but you see, I'm a very conservative person and I don't believe in total integration. If you mean walking hand in hand, and socializing, I'm very cordial. I invite colored people to dinner, colleagues of mine. It didn't matter to me. I wouldn't want them to get married. Of course, that's the thing that everybody says—right away you think they're going to be married! But, they do get married. Let's not kid ourselves; they do get married. And, I don't think colored people want their children to marry whites. If they do, what are they going to do? They can't disown their children, but I don't think they favor that. But, if you mean by integration, our children can go to school together, I don't know why not. I wouldn't mind one bit my grandchildren playing with the black children of the people who live in my building, because they're decent people.

I think it's up to society to see that the black man gets everything that the white man has—earns . . . let me put it that way —earns. I know in city institutions, any new job that's open goes to a black person. Of course, it makes for a great deal of ill feeling, which I can understand, if I go for a job and I'm turned down because I'm white. I want to have the same rights

to a job because I'm white that that girl has because she's black. I don't want to be denied, or if my child is eligible for a scholarship, I don't want him to be denied that scholarship. I think that society can be arranged so that both eligible people can get that job. I have heard somewhere that if a white man and a black man both apply for that job, and even though the white man has children, the black man will get it. I think that's wrong. You know that there is no such thing as having equal qualifications. No two people are equal. So, somebody must be superior. Why shouldn't that be taken into consideration. I don't think that the black man should be given preference. Get rid of those people who say "The teachers are no good, we want only black teachers, we don't want white teachers and Jewish teachers." They think a teacher should be given the job just because he's black. How did the Jewish teacher get there? Because she was Jewish? She never got the job because she was Jewish. She got the job because she went to school and passed an exam, and was appointed. Let me tell you something. When I was graduated from high school, before a teacher could go to training school—they sent speech specialists down to all the high schools to examine the girls. And, if a girl had what was called a Jewish inflection, she never got into training school. If by some fluke, she did manage to get through the net, life was made so miserable for her in training school that she felt like cutting her throat. What's a Jewish inflection? Since I've matured, I hear New Englanders speaking with a rising inflection. It was just that innate anti-Semitism on the part of the establishment that barred these girls, who might have been very good teachers. So, we have come around to a whole new philosophy that the way a person speaks, even though he has a foreign accent, does not necessarily bar him from being a good teacher. Of course we would like teachers to speak English so that the children would be able to speak English the way we think it should be spoken.

Black children don't respond better to black teachers. I think that's the biggest lie. For one thing, the black teachers are much harsher with their children than the white teachers. White teachers wouldn't call the black child names that the black teacher calls them.

Poor schools were not the result of poor teachers and poor teaching. You cannot teach if children are running around the room. You may be God's gift to education. You may be a superior teacher: but you cannot teach if kids are running around the room.

As long as the children are the kind they are now, you will not get the middle class back into the school system. Because, I don't want my children in a room where the teacher has to discipline the children instead of teaching them. Where she has to have a child so close to her for fear that he'll stab or slap somebody in the back, or throw a book at somebody. The middle-class family is right to take their children out of the public schools. You know, when you have a barrel of apples, and one apple is rotten, the whole barrel deteriorates. It's much harder to walk upstairs than downstairs. You want to help these people, but certainly not by exposing your child. You've climbed and pulled yourself up and tried to make something of yourself. Maybe you didn't get where you'd like to be, but why not give your child an opportunity, so that he can fulfill his ambitions, and he'll never

fulfill his ambitions by being surrounded by children who don't have at least as much initiative or at least as much background as your child.

It won't be better if the white mother leaves her child in the school. That won't make it better. It'll be better if you can get the mother of the child now in school to learn what she can do, how she can make her child's life happier. The classes now are almost impossible to manage. We should have fifteen children in the class. We're the richest country in the world, why can't we get it? Why can't we start a crash program of building and renting space in apartment houses? It's been done. The philosophy of the country is not with it. The powers that make our establishment don't want twenty children. They say, "That's like a private school. This is a private school, and we can't give to the public school what we give to the private schools." They have status and they want to keep that disparity. They want to keep that difference. Those people who have it, the people who lay down the rules, they don't want the truth. They don't want to face the realities. I'm beginning to sound like a Communist myself. Just like the mothers of our children are unable to face the realities, they're unable to see that they're failing the children. We have been negligent, and it's no good to say that other people came as immigrants and pulled themselves up. Just because they suffered, doesn't mean these people have to suffer. We've come a long way in our philosophy. The equities have been developed. Humanities have been developed. It's a different world. We have to start fresh. We have to bring to this world this new philosophy that human beings are precious, and we can't do what Hitler did and throw people to the wolves, to the

ovens. We have to try to save the people. Every child whom we save means so much. We've come a long way, and that development should be reflected in our society, and it hasn't been.

If society is going to survive in the hands of militants, it might just as well not survive. I saw a movie about Sweden. Well, this film, showing the life of the young people in Sweden, it tore my heart out. I was hoping that an atom bomb would just descend upon us that very moment and destroy us that very moment. In Sweden, they have the forerunner of all progressive legislation, all progressive housing, progressive ideas, liberal ideas, so we assume that they have a happier life than communities who have more conservative, more rigid, more orthodox ideas. The first scene opens up with a classroom, fifteen-, sixteen-year-olds and a dried up old-maid schoolteacher, who's giving a lesson on sex education. And the children were sitting there rapt. He had illustrative material of the different organs and he was being very specific about everything that takes place. And the kids asked some very telling questions. The movie had the most horrible, devastating, cruel, scenes you've ever seen in your life. All these things are done with the knowledge of the government. The wickedest, the maliciousest, the cruelest, I haven't got adjectives to describe the scenes that took place in this picture. And, that's the life of the young people today. Then they showed a drug scene, of course. If it's happening in Sweden, it's probably happening right here on Third Avenue in the bistros, who knows? I don't know what they want, they say they don't like this world that we've created, and they're going to make a better one. What are they showing us that's better? I don't know.

Well, I will tell you that there will be an exodus of teachers my age in the next two years. The experienced, the old-timers are leaving the school system. Primarily because they can't take the gaff of the militants that say that the teachers are to blame. When we leave the new young teachers can take over. To bring to the children something invaluable. They may not teach in the same manner that we teach, they may be lacking certain know-how, but they have certain other qualities to which the children respond, and I think it's wonderful. I think the youth, the enthusiasm, is very desirable, even more desirable than the maturity and the experience of the older teacher, especially if she only has fifteen pupils. It wouldn't matter if she doesn't have all the routines down pat. If she has only fifteen or twenty children in a room, she can manage to project and give to the children everything that she has learned, almost as successfully, if not as successfully, as the teacher who has gathered from experience little tricks of the trade and ways of doing things to bring results.

I feel the desperation and hopelessness of the situation. I'm not reaching anybody. I sweat blood and try to teach and get no place. I do a day's work and I don't feel the children are profiting. They don't show that they have learned anything. They don't change their behavior. Sometimes I wonder why I stay on the job. Teaching is my way of life. I'm used to getting up in the morning and going to work. But I think I'm going to retire soon. I want to live a more normal life—going to the department stores and being with friends my age.

■ The Boy with the Birds

I always had a sense with animals . . . and birds, especially birds. I wasn't going to go into the business, but some guys wanted to partner up with us. We built a 5' by 5' coop, put a screen around it and started buying pigeons, one at a time. That was the start.

It got to be like a social club up here. Yeah, we used to have a lot of fun, talking and eating. We had a pool table in the hallway and we'd all play and watch the birds winging around.

I don't really love it, but it's a way of staying out of trouble. You know what I mean? Usually there's a lot of trouble on the street and everything that happened either I used to get blamed for, or someone else I hung out with. I guess it's a way of escaping, coming up here all the time. I feel secure this way.

You know, we used to have weight lifting up here? Everything. Friends of friends used to come up when they had nothing to do and we played cards. Then, little by little, everybody started getting older and getting older. They broke away from the crowd. Some started taking drugs. Yeah, I used to come up here and see them taking pot and selling the stuff.

You can't find a good friend in this neighborhood any more. Those other guys, they're taking drugs, smoking and sniffing, but me . . . I'm staying out of it 'cause I used to wind up in trouble just by walking around. But not any more. I was able to resist 'cause I have strong will power. They used to try and bring me in, but I said no, no good. If I take drugs, I'd get a kick out of it, but you still have the problem when you wake up the next morning. That's what I used to say to them. You start with the smallest stuff and you wind up with the most dangerous drug there is.

People around here used to be different and the neighborhood was nice . . . really nice. I don't know what's happened. Maybe it's just that no one cares any more. The policemen don't even care. They used to show up as soon as a crime was committed. Now you call up and they don't show up for hours.

These birds are lucky. They just hatch and fly away. I've been watching them and, you know, the birds, no matter what color each one is, they don't care. That's one thing I've learned from them. They all make love to each other, whatever color they are. I can sit up here all day and watch them together.

■ The Boy with the Guitar

The best thing that happened to me is
my playing the guitar. Really. Like when
I go to sleep I have a song in my mind.
When I'm walking down the street through
all the people I have a song in my mind.
When I'm riding on the trains I have a
song in my mind. All the time.

I like music; I really do. I like it a lot.
And I learned from one of my friends in
the neighborhood . . . by accident really.
I was helping him up the stairway with
the instrument, and he asked me if I
wanted to be in his group. And I said
sure.

■ The Minister

We have a church in a store and we also pray in the homes. It's a Pentecostal church. We know the Bible is the word of God and we know all the Bible says is true.

I became a minister because I like to help the people. The preacher preach to me and I'm convinced. I was going to the congregation when I was seventeen years old and the minister there wanted to make me a minister in that church. When he left they needed another minister and they started to pray to God for someone to help. I knew God needed some men to preach the Gospel, that made me convinced and I start to study the Bible. It takes me a lot of time to know about the Bible. Four years in a school and about nine years all together.

I want to teach because this is the only way the people will do nothing wrong and everything go right: when they believe, and they love everybody. They have a lot of trouble with young people now in the street, drug addicts, all those troubles, we know this is a wrong way to live. We know that the right way to live is making a good condition with God. My congregation is in bad neighborhood, it's not a problem, we like to preach that kind of people, in that kind of neighborhood. We don't try to escape the bad neighborhood. We believe if we preach, God help to take the people out of the condition they are at now, and they start believing in God and looking to God and that way we can have a better community. I believe that this man or that woman belong to God. No matter what condition they are and we try to preach and convince them.

For me, God is the law who create everything in this world and the Bible say one day everybody have to meet God.

We preach to all kinds of guys, Spanish of different countries. The majority is Puerto Rican. I tried about six months ago to make in my church one school, a regular school for the colored people. I can't make it, because I can't speak the language very well. But I think they can live all together like one family because when the people love God, they love everybody. No matter what the people are, they rich, poor or it doesn't matter what kind of people, they have to believe.

No man can give you salvation. No man, nobody, just God. That's what I preach. You believe in a man, it do nothing. You can believe in your friend, but he don't save you. You can believe in your friend for favor; for salvation, you have to believe in God. All the members are poor members, nobody rich. God blessed everybody and they feel happy, they talk to me and they testify that.

They say why they're happy, because God has blessed him that he's found a good job and any way to get money in a right way. And they testify they feel happy the way they help each other. They like to help each other, they want to do more for the church.

Singing is important in our church because you feel happy when you sing. Singing to God. We feel happy. Then after that we preach.

You're lucky if you have a good job. You have time to get rich or get some money, but who doesn't believe in God, he won't become rich. Well, I have my job beside the church. I never take anything from the church. I am a caretaker for eight hours and after hours I work for the church.

In my job, I work from eight to five.

69

From five to six I get home and I shower and look to the home. Then I have to be in church at six o'clock, and I don't come home till after eleven-thirty. Sometimes I find I don't have enough time to be in the house to teach my family. But my wife, she can teach my children. I try to do the best I can, but it's too hard.

There's no salary at all from the church, but I don't want salary from the church because I want to help the church. We have a small congregation now, about thirty or forty members and that's not enough to support one man with a good salary. Maybe one day if the church have more members then I can leave my job and take all the time in the church.

My congregation has grown a little bit but not much. The church is not growing because they tear down too many of the buildings. They start to bring everything down, but we have to stay there and wait. Because we still have some members here, and we can't leave some members. And we believe the city going to make something in this neighborhood, because they have to look for places for the people. Right now when the people looking for an apartment they can't find it. We believe that someday they come back and they going to build something, a big building.

The church going to grow up little by little, maybe today, maybe a couple months more. Sometime we have to take one year to get one or two members.

Maybe in two or three years, the church can support me. In two, three years I know this is big neighborhood again. Every time they can reach one people, we are in victory.

71

4C

■ Apartment 4C

Altogether I had sixteen children. I had eight with my first husband but four died —three miscarriages, and one little girl died from the flu at three months. Then I remarried in 1950 and I have eight more children from my second husband. So now I have twelve children. There are four in the house, two daughters are married and my oldest son lives with his father. Then I have two sons in Rockland State Hospital and three daughters in a foster home. The boys are very sick. I don't know how, but the doctors said they're sick and they are gone since 1954. But soon we'll get a bigger apartment and they can come back with us.

My husband, Ruben, he's on welfare 'cause he's allergic to work. Yes, that's the whole truth and nothing but the truth. When he starts working something always goes wrong and he can't continue working. He's thirty-eight years old and I'm forty-eight. We've been married eighteen years and every once in a while he'll get a job—in factories, pizzerias and restaurants through the years. I tell him he should get a job to help the children but he pays no attention. He's worked for one or two weeks. He's a very irresponsible man. He ain't got nothing in his head.

We moved here last year—about a year and a half ago. We came from Spanish Harlem to the Bronx because I couldn't find an apartment on the East Side. Anyway some of those apartments in Manhattan are as bad as these. In fact the other apartment was in worse condition than this. More holes, more rats and more cockroaches. But we're trying to get a larger apartment. Some are not very big and most of them are in bad condition. It's a problem. You can't go from worst to worst.

74

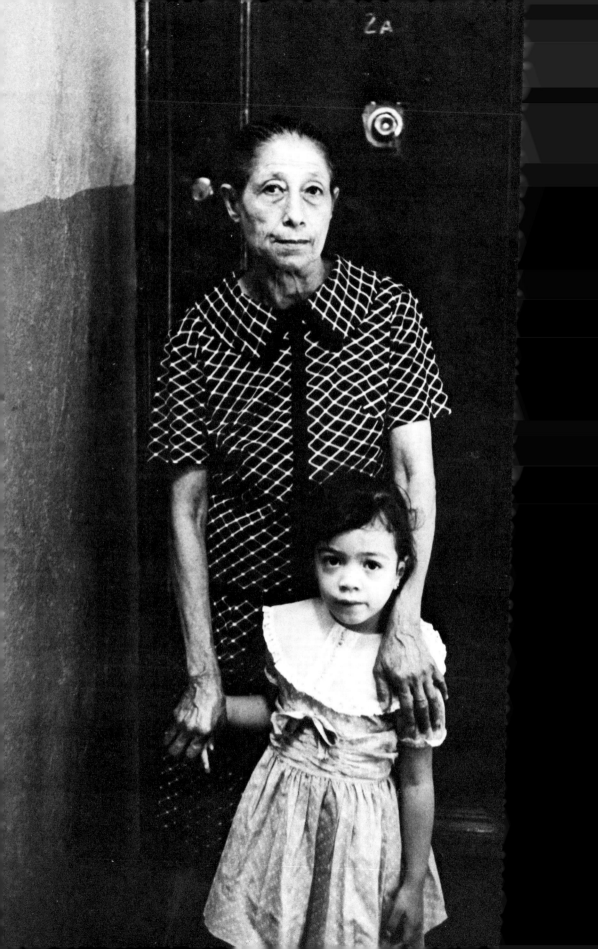

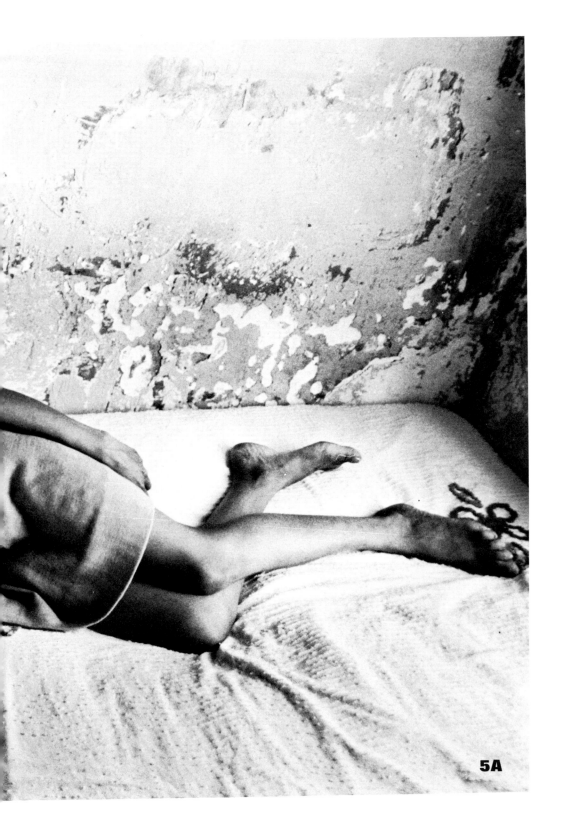

5A

■ Apartment 3C

I'm twenty-five. I've had eight children. My oldest son is dead. He died when he was three weeks old. Since then I've had five children and two miscarriages. It didn't make any sense to me to keep on having children when you're scuffling trying to take care of the ones you've got. You can't provide properly for the ones that you've got. So why keep on bringing them into the world?

Now I don't have to worry about anything like that. Because with the new things that they have now, I mean, if you don't want children you don't have to have them. So I saw the doctor about it and I don't have to have any more, that's it. I mean why keep having children just because you're able to do it? Just keep bringing children into the world and you know they are going to be underprivileged and deprived.

The first one wasn't an abortion. That was a premature baby. The other two I just didn't want them. I just couldn't see how I could afford to have any more children. Well, with the last one I almost died myself. Since that, I've had two children. But after this last baby I went to the doctor, so now I don't have to worry. I don't see how anybody can be against something like that. See, I love my children. I don't want my children to come to me and say, "Mommy, I want some milk." And I don't have a quart of milk because there's nothing in this house to give them. So I know the more I got, the more expensive it will be on me. This don't make no sense. I can't take care of the ones that I got. They're in Puerto Rico with my stepmother.

48

■ Apartment 4B

My name is Crusita Torres. I am twenty years old, and two out of the ten children living in the apartment are mine. Seven of them belong to my sister Luz. She is twenty-five years old. She came from Puerto Rico about ten years ago, but she's too stubborn to learn English. One of the little boys—he's nine years old—belongs to my brother. His mother didn't want him so she gave him to my mother when he was forty days old.

We all live together now. My father— I think he's about eighty—came up in 1967. I take care of him like a baby. My mother came in 1968 with me. She's about sixty-five. She's always saying she's sixty-five, but she doesn't remember what year she was born. In Puerto Rico he cut sugar, and she was a washing-woman, and ironed, and they had their own house.

Luz came to New York in 1959. Our oldest sister was here and she sent Luz the plane ticket. So she came. She married the same year she came and she had six children. Her husband had an upholstery store, but now he's gone. He went back to Puerto Rico with another woman. Luz was three months pregnant. The father of the baby didn't want the baby and was threatening Luz. He wanted her to have an abortion. He said he had enough with two other children he had in Puerto Rico from his first woman, so he didn't want any more children. But he gives ten dollars for the baby.

This apartment is too small for all of us. Welfare wants to break up the two families so we each have our own apartment. This apartment is eighty-two dollars a month for five rooms, all in a row. Welfare gives me a hundred thirty dollars and all that goes for food. The investiga-tor, she knows this so she gives extra money when she sees I have none. So everybody has something to eat. Everything will work out. I don't worry for nothing. Everything always turns out good at the end. My husband goes away, but I don't care about him either. Only my children are important. I want my children to study. But not me—that I never liked. The boy—my brother's boy—isn't in school because he has no clothes. His investigator said that they couldn't give him anything for clothes yet. But it'll be O.K.

I might get a job. I've never had one, you know. Of course with welfare I don't have to kill myself working, but I would like to go out and work to get a break from the kids. I've tried everything else so I would like to try working just to see how it is. Maybe for a week.

■ Apartment 2C

When I was born my age was put in a Bible: August 1902. My father worked in a tobacco factory in North Carolina. We moved there when I was ten years old. When Abraham Lincoln rode through the streets on his horse, my father was ten years old and working at the tobacco factory to take care of his brothers and sisters because his father and mother were dead. You see, my father's mother and father were sold in slavery. My father was born in 1849. My mother was born in 1859. My father died in 1937, and my mother in 1925. She had sixteen children, and I'm the youngest. My father was fifty some years old when I was born. He was eighty-eight years old when he died.

My wife was born in Florida and came to New York when she was about nine

months old. She was raised by her grandfather and grandmother until her grandmother died. Then her grandfather remarried and they bought a home in Long Island, and that's where she was raised. They had their own home and everything. Her mother, you know, was only fourteen years old when she was born, and she was pretty wild. So her grandmother made her grandfather promise to raise her. And that's what they did.

We got married in 1950 in Philadelphia while I was cooking. I'm a cook by trade. I've cooked all over the New York City restaurants. I cooked on a dining car. I was on the Great Lakes, cooking—I ran between Detroit and Minnesota. When we got married I was fifty-two. She was fifteen, just a kid. We lived in Philadelphia for three years but got lonely for New York and returned.

At the time, we were living in deplorable conditions. We would cook a pot of oatmeal in the morning, then reheat it up on the radiator in the afternoon. And you see, we had a trap door on our living room floor. I paid twenty-eight dollars to put something on that floor. Whenever the sewer would back up, all that filth would come up under our floor and run around all over the floor. It was a sewer for the toilets. I mean you could see big turds floating around in the sewer. That's why we moved. One time this went on for four days. My wife had to keep the kids up on the bed. I couldn't let them get down. All that stuff floating around through the apartment until they got the Roto-Rooter man there. And then I had to clean up all that filth.

I hate to complain but I got a rotten deal. We had to move in here in October 1954 because of the sewer in the other apartment. So we got this apartment, it's only on the second floor. And I thought the man promised to fix it up. I thought I was getting a break. Well I thought when he fixed it up it would look halfway decent. But, my God, this place is in deplorable condition and this man keeps raising the rent.

My ceiling is falling down now in the bathroom. They got in there and repaired that ceiling when it was falling down before, about two years ago. They nailed a piece of Beaverboard up there, and then plastered around the side of the Beaverboard and then painted it over. Now it's falling down again. It's a wonder that bathtub don't come through the ceiling from upstairs. And the water has leaked in there ever since we've been here. The pipes up there are rusted. There were no new pipes put in. They are still rusted. And the water runs out of one sink and up into the other one, and stands in the other sink.

In the wintertime we walked around the house with our coats on. We have to put the babies in two pair of pants, long pants and heavy jackets to try to keep them warm. At night when we go to bed, we go to bed with all our clothes on and we put four and five blankets on each bed. I mean it's so cold that when you breathe, you can see the smoke coming from your mouth. I mean, like if you were outside.

We got our two girls sleeping in bunk beds. Our son Manice sleeps in there by himself. I had a crib in there with our two little children, our two babies slept there. But in cold weather, it gets so damn cold up there, with the wind whistling through those windows, that I let them sleep in our only couch with me and my wife. And in the wintertime, when it's real cold, we close off the two bedrooms completely and burn the oven and then we all sleep in here together. I have to put a board and nail it down because I have no connecting doors in this apartment. The only doors are the front door and the door to the cellar. We have no closets in here. Only the one that I bought. I've asked the landlord to put some doors in here for me but he can't find none. One bedroom is supposed to be private for my children; it never has been since I've been here.

One of my babies has been in the hospital twice for lead poisoning. She'd pick plaster and paint and stuff off the walls. It's falling down and she would pick it up and eat it. The baby had gotten so bad, so much lead in her, that she couldn't hold anything in her stomach, even when she drunk water she would bring it back up. The doctor said it was a good thing we got it as quick as we did because, he said, "If she goes into convulsions you're liable to lose her, and she's at that stage right now." They gave her sixteen bottles of that fluid to drive that poison out of her blood. She came back home. We had her home a couple of weeks and we had to carry her back again. The second time we went it was because she had a bean in her ear and they couldn't get it out. But during the time she was in there, they asked me if she had been hospitalized before. And I told them yes and what for. So they checked her blood and they found that she had lead poisoning again. They said that either she had lead poisoning again or that the hospital hadn't gotten it all before. Anyway it had built up to a very high rate.

The reason we haven't moved away from here is because we have five children. It's pretty hard to find a decent place if you got five children. Especially when they are small children. So I've

been running back and forth trying to get a place for us to go, a place to move to. It's kind of a hardship and a handicap here. When we first moved here, I signed a two-year contract and my rent was sixty-four dollars a month. Six months after we moved here, the landlord went to the Housing Authority and they gave him a 15 percent raise. That made me pay seventy-three dollars and sixty cents. They raised my rent nine dollars and sixty cents. When they raised our rent, water was leaking down from the sink all over the pots and pans. The ceiling in the kitchen was all out. Also in the living room, the ceiling was falling and it finally fell in and hit our little girl.

You see, I get a pension. My pension is not adequate to take care of me and my family because we are seven members in this family. So the welfare give me a supplementary check, and they pay the rent. I have been supplementing my pension by working on a golf course. But I can't do that no more. You have to walk six or seven miles in order to make the round of golf. I worked at a big country club up in Westchester. I worked there up to two years ago. I haven't been able to do that no more. I have arthritis, rheumatism and I'm not able to walk with two bags on my shoulders like I used to do. See, I used to make two rounds a day. I made ten dollars a round.

Welfare pays our rent. But I've gone to other places and quite often they tell me they don't want to rent to welfare. They won't take nobody that's on welfare. I walk all over the place. I go to one section and when I cover that I take the bus and come back home. I leave telephone numbers, I fill applications. I look in the newspapers, the agencies. That's another thing I want to tell you. You got something lacking here with the agencies. You've got to pay fifteen dollars to join before you can be available even for them to tell you anything about the place, and even then they lie to you.

I have put in about five or six times for the projects. I went to the Urban League. I've had the welfare to put in for me. I went to the Social Service. They say they can't get a place for anyone. They can't get a place for any welfare recipient. So you got to get out and look for a place yourself.

You go to some places, they don't take welfare. You go to another place, you got too many children. You go to another place, he can't rent it. And if you happen to get lucky and run upon a nice place that you would like to have, and you don't have the money to give to the man, right there . . . why, naturally, if somebody comes along to you with cash, they're going to rent it to that person first.

I've had my investigator tell me that they can find places, but it's no use. He said it wouldn't be worth your bother because the places that the welfare people would place you in would be just as bad as the place you're in now or worse. He said that it'd be better if we get out and find it ourselves. So I guess I'll keep trying.

■ Apartment 3B

I came to New York when I was seven. My mother died when I was two so my father's second wife took me. That's the one I call my mother. She was nice to me and I call her my mother. My father had eight wives, you know. He married the first one and the last one and all the wives took their kids when they were divorced. I lived with them for some years and ran

away from my house when I was fourteen and got married. I've been on my own ever since . . . eleven years.

I moved here, two and a half months ago, because in my other place on Webster Avenue two of the rooms were burned. I had to get out as soon as possible because the smoke was bothering us, so I didn't see this place. I took it at night and he told me he was going to have everything fixed. But the Frigidaire is no good. The toilet doesn't work. The bathtub is very old. I pay here seventy-three dollars a month for four rooms and I pay the gas and the electric. It's not too bad, but I don't like this place. I see all the cockroaches and I can't sleep at night. The cabinets in the kitchen are full of them—even in the stove, you know.

So I'm going to send the twins to Puerto Rico to my mother's house 'cause they're having marks all over their body and I had to put the bottles in the Frigidaire 'cause the little bugs and cockroaches are going all over the food and everything. You know the only thing that I worry here is that they could catch some kind of sickness in the blood. I don't want them to get eaten by the rats and mice that go on the crib. A friend of mine will take the babies to my mother. She has a house and everything. And I'm going to work again. I used to work in a factory in Manhattan, and I want to see if I can get the job back. In a toy factory, stuffing the animals. I closed my case with welfare 'cause I'm going back to work. And my children—they can stay with a friend of mine.

3B

■ Apartment 5C

I am thirty-one years old. I was eighteen when I left Puerto Rico and came to New York. My mother came first and sent for me and we lived together. I was at a bathing-suit factory for five years doing the packaging. Then I was married and had three boys and I quit. My husband was a narcotic. So they put him in jail. So I got divorced and went back to Puerto Rico. I stayed with my grandmother for three years and while I was there I had two more boys. Then I came back because I was in a shoe factory for only twenty-five dollars a week. It was too little. I had to pay ten dollars to my grandmother for the kids and fifteen dollars was not enough.

So I came back. I don't know why. My mother sent me the ticket and she found an apartment for me here in the Bronx and I went on welfare. This was in 1963. I moved to this apartment four months ago. Five rooms for a hundred twenty-four dollars. I have to move again because this apartment is too high—too much rent and not enough room. I have to walk up five flights of stairs. So I'm looking for another one, a big one.

■ Apartment 5B

You feel the first chill and you go and start worrying. That's the main thing that happens in this building. As soon as you feel the first chill then your worries begin. Here comes a winter again. What's going to happen this winter. It ain't like you don't know, 'cause you know. You go through it every year. There's never been no improvement since I've been here. No heat since we've been here. Every winter has been the same. The boiler breaks down for three or four months at a time, or one week we are burning up with steam and the next week we ain't got none. That's right.

I'm sure there is going to be a problem because every year since I've been here —I've been here five years this past September—there hasn't been an improvement. We've had a broken window in our bedroom for nine months now. Thursday the super came up to fix it. But he don't speak no English and I don't speak no Spanish. He was trying to tell me something and I don't know what he's saying and he don't know what I'm saying. So then he called Mr. Gonzalez and he said he couldn't fix it because he had to have some bolts and things and that he had to wait till the Jewish holidays was over because the hardware stores was closed. So far he's never been back up here to fix it.

You know every winter we have to close the two back rooms up. It would be so cold up there. We closed those two rooms up and my husband and I bought a couch and we slept in here, and we put a folding bed in here. We took out the chairs and we put beds in here. The living room looked like one big jungle or something because we had beds all over the

5B

place. We were trying to keep the kids from freezing. We nearly froze anyway, and at one time our gas bill was seventy some odd dollars. It never went under that because that was our only means to get any heat, to burn that stove. We turned that stove on in the morning, and we never turned it off until at night. And when we did turn it off the kids would just freeze. But we were afraid to go to sleep with the gas on, so we turned it off at night. And at six in the morning we would turn every jet on the stove and the oven and that would burn all day long. Sometimes until one o'clock at night. You know we stayed awake as long as possible in order to keep it on.

My little girl, she was born in June of 1965. And the first winter she was here she went into the hospital with bronchitis and pneumonia. My little baby here, she was born in March, and the first winter she had pneumonia. My oldest daughter, Loretta, she had pneumonia since I've been here. I've had three kids with pneumonia in the wintertime. It never happens in the summer. It's always in the wintertime that these kids are in the hospital with pneumonia. No heat.

But considering what we had before, this is like a palace, that's right. More space, with the kids and everything, it's more convenient. Here is 100 percent better than what we had before because then we had only the two rooms. In September of 1964 we moved from 175th Street and Third Avenue where we had only the two rooms. So we were looking for an apartment and we had looked for months and months trying to find an apartment and I end up finding this because this was the only one that I could find. And at that time my mother was the super of this building. We had the same problems

we have now. So there really ain't been no changes.

Even the rent I pay—thirty-four dollars and thirty-nine cents. I'm sure I'm the lowest tenant in the building. You see, I've been here for five years and got help from the welfare because I went to them to get the apartment. They paid the written security. I paid a hundred twenty when I first moved. Sixty dollars rent, and sixty security. And I had been here for about one month, going on two months I would say, and I got a letter from the welfare telling me that I was being overcharged for rent and so I said, "It couldn't be overcharged. Sixty dollars for four rooms." So I didn't bother to go, and then I got another letter telling me that if I didn't come then my check would be held up. So then I went to them, and they told me that my rent was supposed to be thiry-four dollars and thirty-nine cents for this apartment when I moved in here. So far that's all we've been paying.

If we move out of this apartment we would need about six rooms and we can't afford the rent. No, we haven't been looking for no more apartments 'cause I don't get no welfare. Just my husband works and we can't afford to get another one. He works seven days a week. A hundred twenty-five dollars for six days, and on the seventh day he makes about twenty. It sounds like a lot, the words a hundred fifty dollars. You say, "Man, I wish I had that much money." But you don't wish you had it because it ain't nothing when you get through paying bills and things like that. You are lucky if you have the price of a soda left out of that. You pay bills and you got six kids and every time you get your money one of those six kids is going to need something.

You know, my husband hasn't had a

vacation in thirteen years. We don't know what a vacation is. A vacation for us is going to the park on Sundays when he can get off from work, if we can afford it. You know, like during the summer other people take their kids somewhere, but where can we take our kids when he's always working? So I take the kids to the park or something and he can't come with us because he's got to work. If he don't work there is no money. That's the problem. Sometimes I don't think it makes sense for him, too. He could just quit. Many people are walking around here and they ain't doing nothing and they are getting on welfare and they have no problems. Here he works every day, and you ask them to help you get a large apartment for your kids so they won't have to be stuck up like sardines and they give you a big story about it.

A lot of times I argue with him, you know. 'Cause a lot of mornings he would be coughing so bad and he would really be sick and, you know, he leave. And sometimes I would cry 'cause I feel so bad to see, you know, him leaving and knowing that he's sick and should be home. But what can we do? He has to go to work. When he's sick then there is no money coming in unless I go to the welfare and try and get help or something like that. That would be the only way we would make it if he got sick. Our only income is him, you know. Sometimes it all just doesn't make sense. We got married when I was sixteen years old, in 1954, and then we came up here from West Virginia in 1956. I was eighteen when I got to New York City. I'm thirty-one years old and my husband is thirty-five. When we came to New York we had two kids. We thought we would better ourselves by coming up here. But now I don't see where is much

difference. It's the same thing. When we were down there everybody would tell us to come up to New York because they really have good jobs up here. But what they didn't tell us, you know: when you make the good money you've got to spend the good money right away with it. The cost of living is much higher, you know. So it wasn't much difference coming up here if you make a good salary and you spend it trying to keep on living up here. That's the point about it.

You watch TV and you see all these things. All these things my children want. Yeah, but you know you can't get them because it takes money. They show you these things, but they don't tell you how to get the money to get them with. That's the problem. That's just one problem. I figure money is the biggest problem you can have living in the city like this. If you didn't have to worry about the money you wouldn't have no problems. That's the biggest problem I think, money. It's cheaper to live down South but then the work is no good, you know. You don't get no work there. The only kind of work is coal mining.

Even welfare gives no help. Instead of coming in here and saying, "I see you need this and I see you need that," first thing they say is, "You've got to get rid of this and you've got to get rid of that." For instance the beds I bought for my children. At the time I went on the welfare, I can't go to the store and pay seventy or eighty dollars. Even if I could, you know, like get stuff on credit, you know you are going to have to pay more 'cause you are getting it on credit. Well, the average person would go out and say, "Well, I see a set of beds cost seventy dollars, here's seventy dollars, I take the beds." But I can't do that. I don't have that money. So when I go get something I've got to get it on credit and so I have to pay more money to get it. So as soon as the investigator walks in he asks me what my bills are. I tell him, you know, I've got to pay for the beds I've got for the children. And then I showed him the payment book and right away he tells me, "Well, Mrs. Thomas, you know that if you get on the welfare you are going to turn these beds in and we are going to have to give you money to get other ones." So I take away the beds and they send me back fifty dollars to go buy some beds. Where am I going to buy them, in a second-hand store? A rummage sale?

So I'd be better off just making it like I am, than going to them. They are not going to come in here and try to make me live worse than what I'm already living. I've been married to him for thirteen years, and ever since I've been married, he ain't never stop working. Which they should know. I haven't gone to them that often for help. Still, when I go to them for help, the first thing they say, you know, "Well, maybe your husband should do this and do that." I say, "I didn't come to get advice about what my husband should do, 'cause he's got to be doing something. Otherwise how have we been making ends meet all this time." First thing they're going to do is tell him what to do instead of them trying to do something to help what he's trying to do. That's the point that I still don't understand.

They ask you all these questions, all these questions over and over again. You've got to tell them from the time you were born until the present time. O.K. And then when you do need help again, you go to them and you've got to go through the same thing over again. Telling them the history of your life. Every time you go it's the same thing. It don't make sense, 'cause they got a record of this there. So why when you go back to seek help you've got to do the same thing all over again? Why can't they just go back and check your files and see why you were there before? You tell them the truth, so they've got to know the truth, 'cause you probably bring them right to the spot and show them the situation, and they know I'm not lying. So why should I have to go through all this every time I need help?

Really we don't ask for much, you know. We bring up our kids, the best we can. We don't ask for much. I've seen people, they've got Cadillacs and are on welfare. That's right. Cadillacs and a little of everything else, they've got. We've got nothing. And my husband's been working like a dog for thirteen years. Seven days a week is all he can work. It's all he can do.

■ Apartment 5D

You know, like I went to the welfare once and this man said right away, "Have you ever taken any birth control?" And I told him no. "But why? You know under the circumstances it's hard to take care of a family." If I want to take something to stop having children I think it should be up to me. I don't think nobody in this world has the right to tell me that I can't have children. And then if I know I can't afford them I don't think it's their right to tell me. And right away when he told me I let him know that. So if it hurts me, I don't care. I don't think they got the right to tell me to take something. That's the way I feel about it. When you take this stuff you ain't got no guarantee what this stuff is doing to the inside of you noway. They have never been sure that this stuff can't hurt you one way or another. They had out the pill and they had out a big article about the pills giving you cancer. Yet they still got the nerve to try and pump this into people's head to take it. And right back they backtrack and tell you that it will kill you if you do take it. So what are you supposed to do? I think there should be a law against them trying to force this stuff on people. I figure, if you want to take it, it's your life, you do what you want to do. If you don't want to take it there is nobody that has the right to force it on you.

I think that's a lousy way of saving the city money is to stop the people from having kids. That's the point I don't understand. The very leaders that we got now. If their mothers didn't have them how would we have them to lead us and now they don't want us to have kids. Maybe our kids could come up and be a leader some day too. So where would they be at, if their mothers were taking pills to stop them from being born. They should think about that, I think. They don't complain about others because they don't have to take care of them but they figure we have them and they are going to have to take care of them. That's the point. All these rich people, they could have a thousand of them. The more that come, the more they think they are going to give them. Poor people don't have kids, rich people have them.

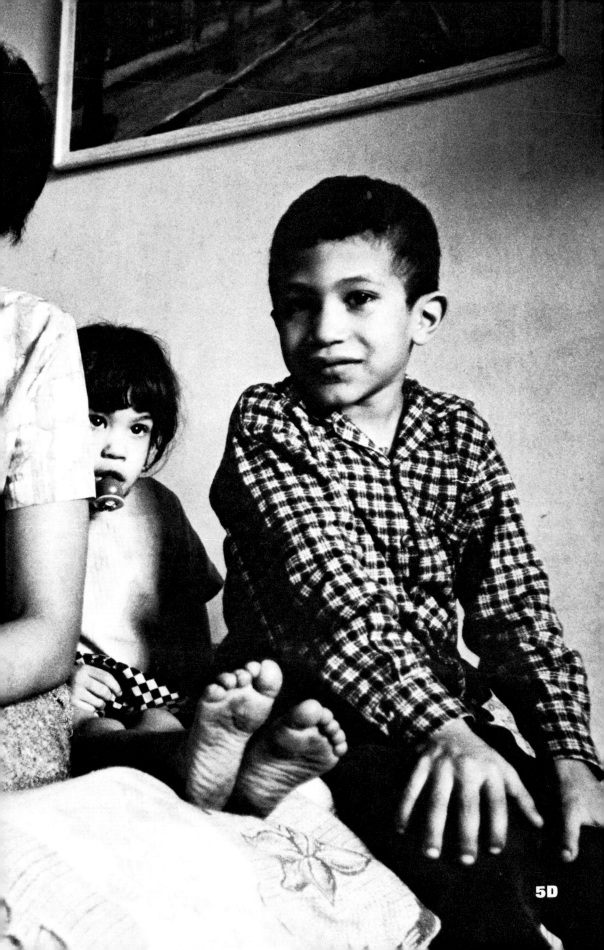

Geneva

■ Geneva

I was born in Savannah, Georgia, in 1951. My mother and my aunts were living together in something like an apartment building. A two-family house, they called it. My mother says she had a hard time there. You know, there wasn't hardly enough food for us, and she'd take food off her plate to give to us. It's just that we had financial problems. That's all. Like money problems. We ran short of money sometimes, ran short of food sometimes, and stuff like that. Still the same thing. The baby run out of diapers. So it's just financial problems. That's all. It's a big problem, but we manage. Anyway, you know, we do the best we can. Like we borrow money. I don't know nothing much about it—about where my mother got money. I just know what they tell me. And they don't tell me nothing 'cause they say I talk too much. All I know is we came to the city here in 1955 and I was only four. We came up here, but mostly they stayed in Savannah. My aunts and uncles, cousins, nephews, nieces—they're all in Savannah.

But we came up to improve our life, you know. Up here we lived in different places before we came to the Bronx, three or four different places—117th Street and Jefferson Place; 155th Street, Washington Heights; Third Avenue and 177th Street. I don't know why we moved so much. I guess we was trying to get a better place, you know. On 177th Street the man didn't want to fix the door, so we moved. It was nice up there, though. Nice neighborhood, nice and clean and everything. The man just didn't want to fix the door, so we left.

I was attending the Dodge High School on Southern Boulevard in the Bronx. Tak-ing the bus, the number 19. Took me straight to Dodge. Then I switched to Roosevelt High, but I didn't finish. I was in the eleventh grade there when I dropped out. Time for my baby. You know, James. My mother didn't say too much about it. She just, you know, she wanted me to go and finish school and make something out of myself. But it was done, and what could she do. She cried a lot. She wanted me to take up my nursing training and make something out of my life. She just said she was going to help me. That she was going to go all the way with me, that's all.

I didn't tell none of my friends 'cause I don't have friends. I have acquaintances. I didn't tell none of them. Bonnie knew. But I didn't tell nobody else. I told the school in my fifth month I was going down South to a funeral. In September 1967. And I never came back. I guess they think I'm still down South at the funeral.

I felt guilty in a way, you know, 'cause I knew what I was doing then, and I was making a second mistake all over again. With Theresa, I didn't know what I was doing then. I was young, even younger. You know, my mother had explained everything to me, but I didn't take heed to it until I got Theresa, I guess. I was going to Dodge then. And I went to school through the whole nine months. I didn't start showing until I got to my last month. We got out June the 27th in 1966 and on the 28th Theresa was born. The school wrote and said I could come back 'cause my mother went and explained to them. So they still promoted me and gave me my award for attendance and my certifi-cate and everything. Nobody knew any-thing 'cause I went to a doctor at seven o'clock at night. Until I had the baby.

That's when everybody found out.

I got a summer job then. I was working in a recreation center part-time and I was working in the hospital as a dietician aid. Two jobs. I just did it 'cause I was healthy enough. Theresa was about a month old and my mother took care of her. I got the job at the recreation center at a public school. They wanted some older person to mind the younger children in the playground. So I just watched them. And I got paid for it—$34.78. Then we moved after the summer. I was fifteen then. And I got a job at Parkchester Hospital, as a dietician aid. After a month or so I went back to school. I got out at two o'clock and I worked from three to seven. But I quit work. I just didn't like it.

I went to Roosevelt that year. Then in September 1967 I got pregnant again—with James—and I dropped out. My mother took that harder—than the first time, I mean. But now I'm going to school at night—back in Roosevelt. 'Cause I want to work during the day. But I liked school. I liked it a lot. And I was very smart in school. If I'm interested, I'll do my work. If I don't want to be bothered, I don't want to do nothing. When a subject gets boring, I don't want to do my work. But when a test comes, I would do the test 'cause I know that's what really counts. I always do my homework, but in school I'd be reading comic books. I was like the teacher's pet, you know. I would do my homework and everything, and help the teacher out—that way he could have something good to say about me. I was very good in school. I never had no bad conduct marks. And my attendance was good, and I never hardly came late. I used to cry if I had to stay home. If I was sick, I had to stay home, I would cry to go to school.

Me and my brother John's two different people, you know. I do what I want to do, he do what he wants to do. I always loved to go to school. Then as I grew older, I got tired. Then I dropped out to have the baby, so I wanted to go back to school, but I said I'll finish in night school. I only have a month and another year to finish anyway.

To get my education. That's what I want to do. That way when I was small, I'd say, "Oh, mom, I want to go to school. We got to go to library today," or something like that, or go to gym. But now that I grew older, and was in high school, I had experienced everything from elementary through high, and I was on my own—changing classes, going to gym, undressing and stuff like that. In elementary, you just play games and jump rope. You wouldn't be changing into gym suits, and taking tests. So I miss it. The only thing important is getting an education out of school. It's not fun no more to me, just going to school every day, learning. When I was small, I thought it was fun going to school. Just getting up every morning, getting dressed, and going to school was a whole lot of fun. Jumping rope. But now that I got older, I learned that school is more than just going to school having fun. It's for you to get your education. And that's all. I'm going to night school to get my education. When I was young, I wasn't thinking about education, I was . . . just one thing crossing my mind—getting up early in the morning, going to school. I got fun getting up early in the morning and going to school.

Now I just want to finish school. That's just my ambition. I want to finish school and make something out of my life, 'cause I got to get a job that's making some money. Nursing, that's what my ambition

101

is. I want to be a nurse. A registered nurse. I enjoy helping people, you know, that can't help themselves.

But I got these two kids to take care of, and that might make it hard. One father helps a little, the other don't. Now, Theresa's father—Junior—he's nineteen. Him and his mother take care of the baby. He's glad to be a father. He comes to see Theresa. Buys her clothes. He gave her a birthday party. Him and his mother mostly come on the weekends, but I don't talk to him that much. He just come over, see the baby, and then he leaves. He's nice and everything, but he acts like a baby himself. You know, he don't act his age. He acts like, you know, a thirteen-year-old kid. He's immature. Very immature. I don't know how I got involved with him. I guess 'cause I was young and didn't know no better. I was only fifteen.

Now, Eddie—that's James' father—he's different. He knows what's going on. He knows a whole lot, to be his age. He's twenty. I liked him. When I got pregnant, I knew everything that I was doing! And he knew everything that he was doing. I knew about pills and stuff. I knew all about that. I wanted the baby. That's why I had it, 'cause I wanted it. I just felt I wanted something that was part of him. And no matter how things turned out, I'd still have something that was part of him. That's all. I liked him, yeah. I hate him now, I guess. 'Cause he got married on me! God!

He asked my mother to marry me, but my mother didn't like him . . . like he wouldn't keep a job or nothing like that, so my mother figured that he wasn't capable of taking care of me and the children, so she said no, so then Eddie married this junkie. After all I been through! God! The boy I liked a whole lot

got married on me. Now, Eddie, he was a hustler and a pimp. He called himself a hustler—go out and gamble, shoot dice and stuff like that. Mug people, snatch pocketbooks, stuff like that. I didn't know till after. When I met him he had a job at Horn & Hardart's restaurant. He was nice, and then when I was going with him about a year, and I got pregnant . . . in nine months he just changed.

Then he comes to the hospital—and he brings this girl, this junkie, with him. I didn't want to cry. I was just so mad I wanted to hit both of them. I just sat there. I wasn't afraid. You know, like I went through it before, but I missed my mother and everybody at home. I just felt lonely. My mother came to see me every day in the afternoon and morning, but I knew she had the kids home to take care of. I still felt lonely; it was boring. Nothing to do. Get tired of laying in bed sleeping. And then Eddie comes with this girl. I was mad! I'm sitting up there having his child, and he's going to come and bring another woman to see me, you know. I could have died on the table, the baby could have died.

After that, wherever I saw Eddie I'd ask him for some money. I don't care if James had twelve pairs of diapers, I would always ask him for some money. He gave it to me, too. He better give it to me! I'd curse him out on the street! I would if he didn't give me no money. And he be up at his mother's house, and his wife would be sitting down drinking and having fun, I'd walk in and I'd say, "Eddie, James needs some diapers and some food, and I don't have no money." He'd go in his pocket and give me some money. I'd see him on the corner, I'd say, "Eddie, James needs so-and-so," he'd give me some money. He'd say, "Damn! Every

time you see me you need some money." I said, "That's right! You had him. You going to take care of him!" That's why he figure he mad at me. One time when I got mad I said, "I'm going to take you to court and press charges against you." But I was just fooling. He laughed it off. He knew I wasn't going to do it. And he was good to the baby.

He'd change the baby's diapers sometimes. James would mess and Eddie would get a washcloth. 'Cause I know one night I was so sleepy, I think I was sick. Yeah, I was sick—I had cramps—and Eddie came up there knocking on the door. So my brother let him in. So he went in the room and James start crying. James was about three weeks old. He had messed in his clothes, all over his diaper and undershirt. So Eddie sat there just as nice, and gave him a bath and put him on clean clothes, and then he left. He locked the door behind him and left. And then one day he came up again, and ironed all James' clothes. His wife got mad though. She said, "Get your butt downstairs!"

Then one day he came up, and he said, "How's the baby?" And I said, "Fine." I said, "He got a drawer full of clothes need ironing." He said, "Why you haven't ironed them?" I said, "I'm not supposed to do it. You supposed to do it." So he took all the clothes out, and he ironed every last one of them. And his wife came up there. She was mad. So they left together. He finished ironing his shirts, and he left. He ironed every single one—diapers, undershirts and everything. I wasn't going to help him! I sat there smoking my cigarette and looking at him. That's about all. He ironed every last one of them. He seems a whole lot concerned. 'Cause he wanted a boy. And he wanted

a child so bad, I guess, since that was his first one.

Now then, when I heard Eddie was robbing some grocery store, and killed this man—Hector Torres—I just couldn't believe it. I was shocked, you know. I say, "Murder? No, not Eddie." Then I picked up the paper and I saw it. And my mother couldn't believe it either. She don't like Eddie, but she couldn't believe it. And John—he hung around with Eddie—he couldn't believe it. I can't see Eddie doing something like that. Killing that man in a grocery store. If nobody couldn't tell me different, I would swear he was framed or something.

He was strong—like he was the best fighter around there. Maybe he would steal or something like that—'cause he had a record for stealing and stuff like that or getting caught with stolen goods. But when it come down to robbery and murder, I just couldn't believe it, boy! He had a very soft heart. He don't like to hurt nobody's feelings. But then they say Eddie and this Lopez character robbed this store of nine hundred dollars and killed this guy.

Eddie had come around to see the baby. He said, "I won't be able to see the baby any more." He said, "Here. Take this money and buy the baby some carriage and some clothes, and some food." He didn't say why. He said, "Tell the baby I'm his father. Even though you hate me." He always said that every time he seen me, so I just didn't pay him no mind. I took the money and I bought the carriage. I saw him the next day, and I gave him the receipt. He said, "What do I need that for?" I said, "I'm showing you how much I paid for it." He said, "I don't need that. I know you going to buy for the baby. At least I know that much of you,

106

that you take care of your child." I said, "Give me ten more dollars then." He gave me ten. I said, "You working or something, you got all this money?" He said, "You'd be surprised what I do." I said, "Yeah, I bet I'd be surprised." And when I saw that paper about the murder, I was surprised!

So now Eddie is in prison and I've got my two children and I'm going to get out and work hard enough to take care of them. I don't think I need no man to help me. 'Cause now I'm experienced through twice. I don't think I need any man to help me. If I want to raise my children right—if I want to get things for them—I have to get out on my own. I can't depend on nobody. That's the way I like it. So I want to get a job. And I want to finish school. When I was waiting for the second baby I was taking high school equivalency at home. I did it 'cause during my spare time I could be doing something that would help me when I go back to school. I saw it in a newspaper or a comic book. Two dollars a month. So I took it and then I discontinued it when I went back to night school, so they just sent me a blue certificate that I was taking it.

See, I don't need a man. I'd rather stay by myself. It's not I don't trust men. I just don't feel like being bothered. 'Cause sometime I get lazy, and I cook dinner when I get hungry. And I have to rush, and you know, "My husband coming home, let me cook dinner." Now I cook it when I get ready to cook. I clean up when I'm ready to clean. I don't think I'll never get married. For the children, I'm the mother and the father. I don't need no man. I think I can do just as good as a man can. I just tell them who was their father and forget it. No sense in hiding it from them. Let them know the facts, that's

all. Just like if the father died. Now I just want a job that makes some money, and take care of my children.

That's why I was so excited when I passed the test for the job at the telephone company. I wanted the job then. So then this woman told me that my baby wasn't old enough, and that I'd have to come back when my baby gets old enough. So it hurt me 'cause I wanted to work then and there. I didn't want to wait for November. She says to come back and I'd get the job right away. But I wanted it then. What did the baby have to do with it? It's me that's working, you know. Why should the baby have to be a certain month old before you can work. It don't make sense. I was mad. So tears was coming out of my eyes, that's all. I wasn't straight-out crying. I wanted to work then, I didn't want to wait for November. And then when November came, I didn't want it. 'Cause I had another job. I could have gone back, and they be paying more, but I just didn't want it. I felt this way. If I couldn't get it then and there, I didn't want it at all.

I'm in a training program now. It trains young dropouts and old people about thirty or forty to be secretary-clerks, and telephone answerers and everything like that. Train you to work for an insurance company. You learn how to file, type, answer phones, stuff like that. I like it very much. I get $64.84 a week. The whole training program is seventeen weeks long, and they give us a raise December 18, so when we get to Metropolitan we make about $76.00 or something like that.

It's better than nothing, but it's not that much. And then if you good at typing, you can move up to IBM machines, and you can move up to a high position, and get a raise every four months. If you're

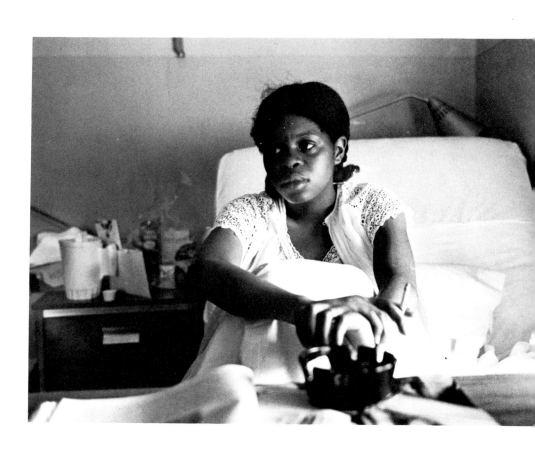

good. But if you don't change your ability, then you get the raise as it comes. I'm taking nursing while I'm working. I'm going to night school. After I get my diploma, I'm going to take an academic diploma, and after I get my academic diploma, I'm going to go two years to nursing school, and then I'll start my training, if I pass all the tests. I want to be a registered nurse. That's what I want to be.

And I'd like to get my mother off Third Avenue and get her in a nice apartment and furnish it. And I want to get my own apartment. I mean I got to get my own apartment. One thing is in my own apartment Theresa would know I'm her mother, 'cause she'd be with me at the nighttime, you know. She'd understand that my mother's her grandmother, not her mother. Now she thinks I'm her sister. She calls me "Gene"! I want her to call me "Mother." It makes me feel good that my mother takes care of Theresa and James, you know, that she cares so much about them, she pays them some mind. She keeps the kids while I go out, and while I work, and she buys them clothes like they were her own kids. She loves them. But I want them to know I'm their mother.

Then I want to get out of this block because it's filthy. It's too filthy. Just too filthy to raise children. A child can pick up a disease or something. People just throw garbage out the window and the garbage men don't bother about coming collecting it. My mother make us take our garbage down and put it in the garbage can, but people throw refrigerators out the windows, dirty old bedsprings, messy diapers, and stuff like that. Don't make no sense.

It must be the Spanish people, 'cause when we moved in the lot was so clean, you know. And then about two or three weeks later the yard was full of garbage. It looked like the Sanitation Department. And they used to come around regular and clean the lot out. But it don't make sense if they're going to keep throwing it out . . . they must enjoy it! It's just filthy, that's all. My mother signed a petition, and I signed. But it's still filthy. Some people don't even live around here. They come from all the way round the corner and throw garbage in there.

And there are rats. I used to see them every day. You can hear them in the night. They be in the kitchen, and you come in the kitchen and they run down the hall. Then Theresa was bitten. Her ear swollen up. She had to stay in the hospital for three weeks for an operation on her ear.

I want to get out of this neighborhood. It's too filthy around here to raise children, and like sometimes you see people on the street eating out of garbage cans. Like the other day I see this man. He didn't look like a bum, you know, but it looked like candy he was taking out of the garbage cans and everything. So it was my last fifty cents, but I gave it to him. I said, "Don't eat out of garbage cans." And he said "thank you" and walked away. It doesn't matter to me that it was my last fifty cents, but it makes me sad and mad for him eating out of the garbage can. If that was someone in my family, I'd appreciate it if somebody walk up to him and give him a quarter or something to buy him something to eat.

It's sad and filthy here. Garbage and junkies and everything. Of course, living in a neighborhood with all this, it's best to know somebody. Know the junkies, and the reefer smokers, and all that. That way,

110

when they see you walking down the street and somebody else want to rob you, they can say, "No, man. I know her. She's very nice. Don't do that." 'Cause like a junkie, he knows what he's doing. Like he be high, but he know you. If he meets you one day, he know you the next day. 'Cause they intelligent that way.

I just want to raise my children, buy them some clothes, and put them in school. Then I'll work every day, take care of my little brother. That's about all. I have dreams about it, but you know dreams don't never come true.

I have beautiful dreams, though. Like I dreamed one time that I was rich, and I gave my mother her own place, and I had my own place too. It's just funny, you know. I dreamed a whole lot. Like I dreamed that I was going to find some money, and the next day when I come outside, I be looking on the ground for money. I do. I be just looking for money. But money's not everything. But you got to have money to get what you want.

I have this picture of how I want my house to be. This is what I dreamed my house was going to look like. A really fabulous place, that's all. I want four rooms, I want a nice living room. I want a stereo. I want a black and white hi-fi TV. I want carpets on my floor. I want floor mats. I want a whole lot. I want a bar. I just want a whole lot. And I want a bedroom set. I want my children to have a bedroom set. I want a nice kitchen, with them brown cupboards, cabinets, and stuff like that. And I want a tiled bathroom. That's all. That's four rooms right there.

Once, I had a dream about myself and my children. I consider myself as grown now, but like I grew up and learned more than I learned now. Like I finally found the right man for me, and he took care of me and my kids, and he asked me to marry him. So I married him. He bought me a nice home and everything. And we had money in the bank, we had a car, our children had what they needed, and I had what I needed. I dreamed that we were both happy together. Had a fine apartment. So every Sunday we would invite my mother over for dinner. Then I didn't like where my mother was living, so we saved enough money and bought her her own apartment with my brother, my little brother Larry. I know she was happy. As long as she's happy, I'm happy. So every Sunday she would come over to my house and have dinner. She was proud of me, and I was proud of her, for what I was doing to her and what she was doing to me. She took care of my kids while I was young, and I was showing her, as I got older, how I appreciated it.

And I dreamed that my brothers would come over and stay with me sometimes. And we would go out together, party, have a nice time, and they'd go home, and I would go home. I dreamed that I had a wonderful marriage, and everything was going right for me. I just hope the dream come true, that's all. But dreams don't come true. So I just stay by myself. I don't need nobody. I just take care of myself and my children.

I guess dreams don't come true. Still I want to get my own apartment and I got to get a job that pays some money and take care of my children.

You know, there's a lot going on that I don't understand. All these rich people, they got all the money, but yet there's slum areas, and stuff like that, and they say they building and rebuilding. You see them tearing down, but you hardly

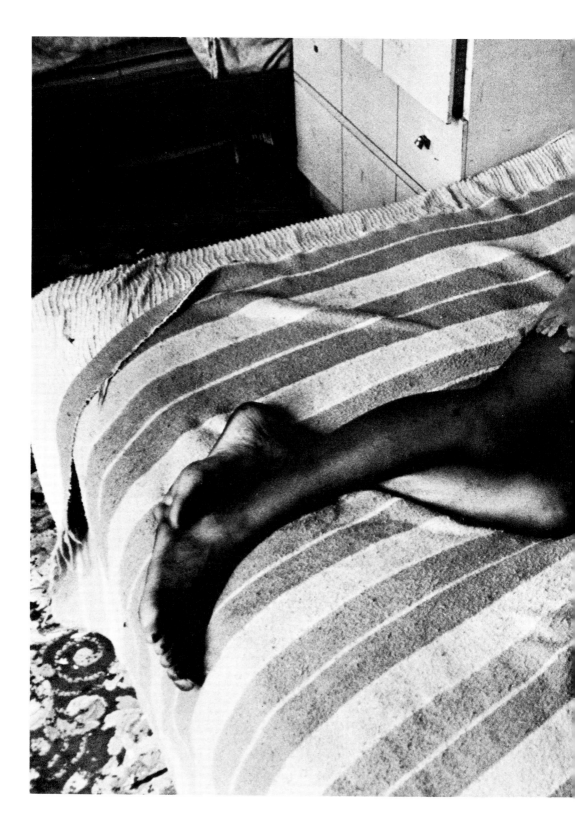

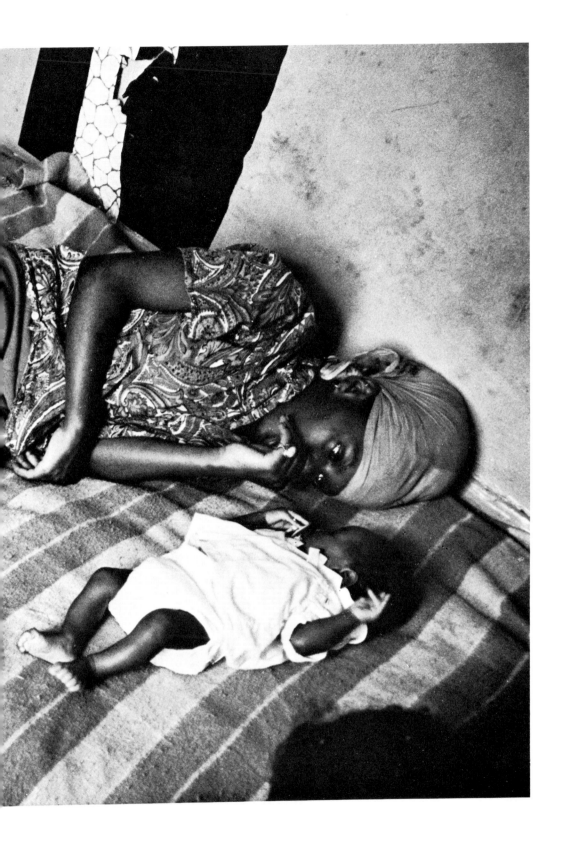

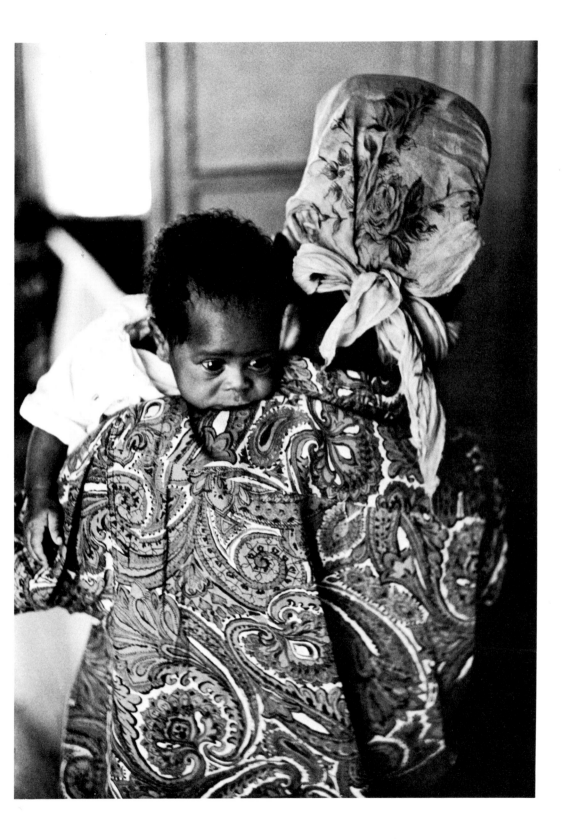

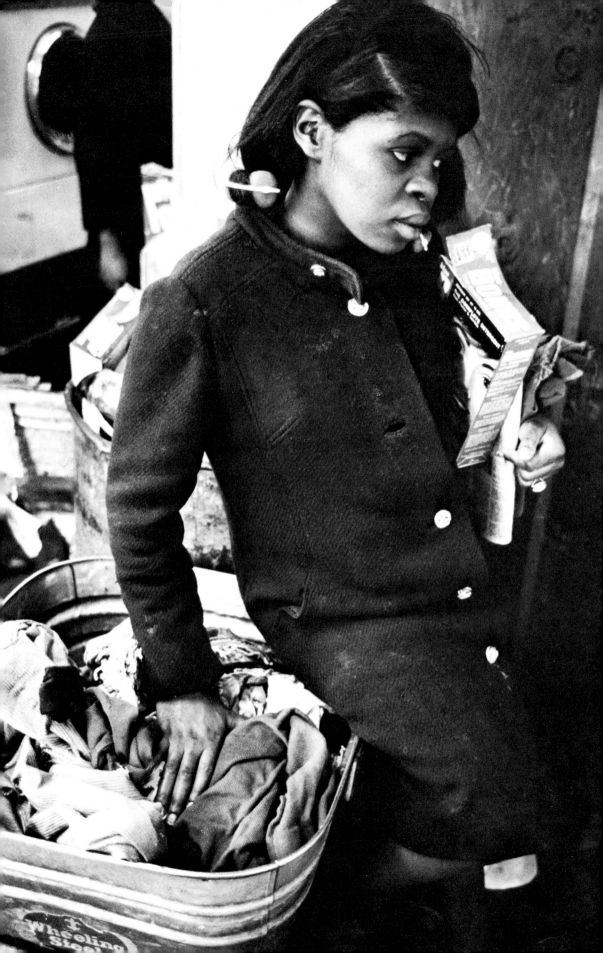

see no buildings coming up. You see more tore-down buildings than you see any building that's coming up. And the buildings they are remodeling, Negroes can hardly get in 'cause the prices are so high. It don't make no sense. If they building it for the slum areas they should make the prices lower. You have to go through all this stuff just to get in the building. Like my cousin. He had just came from Vietnam, and Uncle Sam had gave him a letter. He still got to go to Vietnam and then come back and get a job, but he can't get the apartment and now he don't want it, 'cause he tired of going around and around in circles.

You see, even though we dropouts and stuff like that, we ought to get a job making some money. Probably wouldn't be so many people on welfare. There's a whole lot of old people here who dropped out of school. Now they get a job making thirty or forty dollars. That's not money. That's not even enough money to get them what they want. That can't even buy food to last them. And yet they wonder why there's people on welfare. They should just sit down and think.

Another thing that don't make sense is prejudice. Like I got on the train one morning, and this white lady, she was holding on to the strap, and I put my hand up there, and she moved away. So, like when she moved away, I promptly pushed her down, and she looked at me like I was stupid. It don't make sense. They knew there's a whole lot of Negroes that are going to be going to work on the train, or going shopping, and they act like they don't want to be near them. Then one night I was coming home, and there was this white lady on the train, and she says, "All the black people come from Africa, and they live like dogs.

Dogs live better than them. They wouldn't be over here if it wasn't for us. We brought them over here and we was using them to clean our house and everything." So it made me mad and I started cursing and everything. So then a cop came up to me and said, "Is there any problem?" I said, "You'd better get this lady off the train before she get hurt!" She was still cursing. I went to hit her, and the cop grabbed my hand and told me that wouldn't be right. He put the lady off at the next stop.

I guess there's a whole lot of prejudiced people in the world. But they should know that Negroes are going to be on the train or restaurants—wherever they go, Negroes are going to be. There's just as many Negroes as there is whites in the city. To me it's stupid to be prejudiced. Everybody's human. 'Cept they just different colors, that's all. If you cut a white person, he going to bleed. If you cut a Negro, he going to bleed. So I don't see the difference. Just the skin is different, that's all.

When I was going to school—I was going to P.S. 98—and like I was the only colored; not the only colored in the school, but to me it seemed like it, 'cause there were so many whites, and like I was always the only colored in all my classes, from third grade to sixth grade. So one day this white girl and this other girl was fighting and I was trying to stop the fight. So she called me a black nigger, and she hit me. We started fighting, and all of a sudden she started crying, "I can't breathe, I'm going to die, I have bad heart trouble," and all this. I wouldn't let her go, and kept choking her and choking her and choking her. So the principal came out, and he grabbed me and he took us to the office, and he called my mother, and he said that he was going to

117

leave me back, 'cause I had no business hitting her back, even though she hit me, I had no business hitting her back. But my mother explained to him that she raised us so that if somebody hit us, we was supposed to hit him back. He was on the white child's side. He wasn't on my side, 'cause I was black. He was going to leave me back, but he was going to put her up in her grade. So he said, "All right. I'll leave both of you back," after my mother raised a little sand. So she started crying, and I didn't cry, so he said, "What's wrong with you? You don't care if you get left back?" I said, "No. 'Cause either way, as long as I know I'm smart, and I pass my work, you don't have no reason to hold me back." So he said, "That's true." And he said, "Well, I'll put you in sixth grade on trial, and if you don't do good, then I'll put you back in fifth." So he put me in sixth grade, and he skipped me all the way to seventh grade. Then from seventh grade, I got skipped to ninth.

There's plenty prejudice now. And I don't think the world is going to get any better, 'cause there's always going to be prejudice. I think the world is going to get worse, if you want to know the truth. You can see right now. You don't see nothing progressing. They started programs. All right. The programs are going along well. I'd say I give them about two more years and they going to cut the programs out. Something's going to happen. And they still killing and robbing and going on. And you see crooked cops out here. There's more crooked cops out here than there's people.

You see that every day.

How's the world going to get better when you have cops out here that's doing the same thing that people are doing?

In order for the world to get better, you got to have people that you can trust. And there's nobody that you can trust, 'cause there's a crooked cop. Now, the cop is going to pick up somebody. They pay him off, he got money in his pocket, and he come back and tell them something else. They doing just like the regular people doing. Mugging and killing each other. That's why so many cops dying. Nobody trusts cops no more. And they throwing rocks and bricks at the firemen.

Then there's the fact that the white man going to always own everything. We don't own nothing. The white man own everything. They scared to give one Negro power. 'Cause when one Negro gets power, that means all going to get power. And they sure don't want the Negro to take over. They probably feel sorry for having us for slaves, stuff like that, so they say they going to give us jobs and houses, and treat us nice. But you come down to power—they got it and they afraid we going to get it. Now, the Muslims and the Panthers and the Five-percenters, they fighting for freedom. But we got freedom—we're just slaves: we can do what we want without asking some master, but we don't got power.

And they can destroy us if they want. When Uncle Sam gets ready he can destroy the black man if he want to. The white man has the Army, the Navy, the Air Force. What do the colored people have? They don't have no armed forces or nothing.

It's more their country than ours. It was the Indian's country when the white man came and bought it from the Indian. And then they went into Africa and brought us back in slavery. Brought us over here to work 'cause a white man couldn't do his labor. He would rather let a Negro do it

119

'cause he was stronger. He knew a Negro would stay in the sun. They going to last longer. They say, "We going out to get us a couple of those black people that are stronger. We know we can send them back if they don't do their work."

Well, at least Martin Luther King had respect. He was doing something. He was making marches to tell people what we need, and what we really want. But the Black Panthers and the Muslims, they out there destroying the white people, having fights, causing trouble, winding up in jail. That don't make no sense. That's stupid. They should just speak and tell; why use violence? There's enough of that. They supposed to be fighting for freedom. They don't have to go out there and fight and mug everybody. And they talking about they want civilization in the world. But they killing each other. They say they're not here to destroy. They're here to build. All right, why they destroying and trying to build? They can't do both.

Now, for me, I'd like to see people talk together, being honest with themselves and honest to other people. I feel if some-body don't like me, I'd rather for them to tell me. Why sit there and pretend? Come out and tell me. If you don't like me, you don't like me. If I bother you, let me know. That's how I feel. If you don't like me, well, we don't have nothing in common. There won't be no argument or nothing, 'cause you know she don't like you, then that's the best way to be. There wouldn't be so much killing going on. 'Cause we'd have a better understanding of each other, there wouldn't be so much killing and mugging going on. Then we'd sit down and really have a conversation about what life was really about, and we'd understand each other.

Someday I'm going to have to explain this world to Theresa and James.

I would tell them to believe in God. God is just something that's up in heaven watching everything that they do. He's got his book down here for you to read. He know you not going to obey every commandment, but he got it there for you to read, and understand what everything means. Try to go by His words. I believe there's a God up there, but nobody knows what color he is. There's only one God, and nobody's ever seen Him. Everybody else believes in different gods—like Allah, and statues and stuff like that. Everybody has their own beliefs too. You just got to do the best you can . . .

I would tell them that the world is bad, and it don't make sense for them to get out there and make it no worse. This world is big, and you have to take a whole lot. Even if you don't want to. If somebody hit you, just walk away. Everybody's the same. If you cut a white man, he going to bleed. If you cut a Negro, he going to bleed. He shouldn't hate nobody, or dislike somebody. If he dislike somebody, don't be with them. Don't even socialize with them. That way, stay by yourself if you don't like nobody. And don't ever come out and call a man against his race. "You white so-and-so" like that. Doesn't make sense. 'Cause we're all equal to one. Both human. That's what I would tell them. I would tell them to try to get along with everybody. That's all. And make the world better. Even though there's somebody that don't want to be bothered with you, you don't have to be bothered with them. You can meet some nice people. There's some really nice people out there. You just have to wait and see, that's all. I'd tell my children don't go around starting trouble.

120

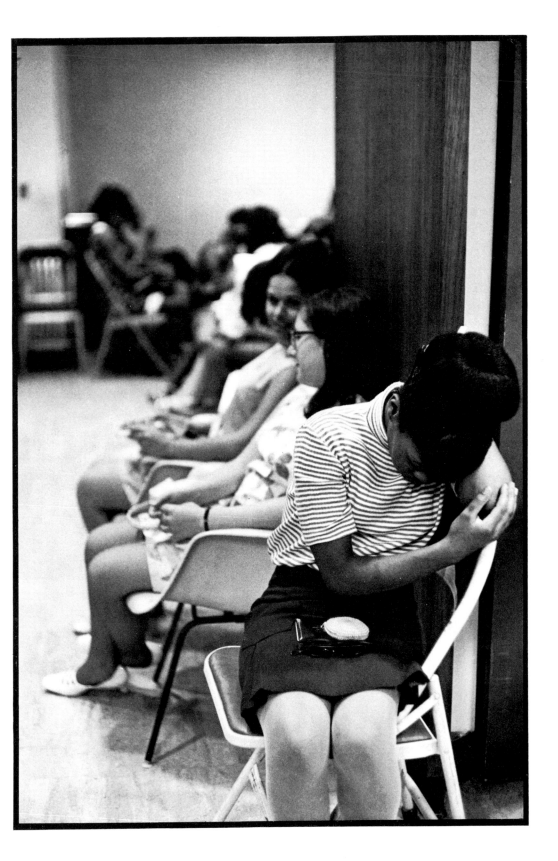

John

■ John

Now the big question is, Who is John Smith? John Smith is a black man, which means his life is based on himself. He had to make it himself without help. Just coming out and saying "He's a black man"—well, most likely people feel he's only another nigger out in the street; he's dumb, ignorant and he doesn't know no better. Well, speaking of John Smith, you would have to say there was nothing that was gave to him, he had to make it himself. My life has gone through hell trying to get the kind of things that other people have and you want, and how to go about and get it. That's the problem. How to get something that you ain't got and have to go and hustle it.

I was going to write a book about myself, called *Time and Matter*. Well, this is the way I started it. You know, like what about if you were John Smith, right? Place of birth: Harlem Hospital. Date: August 2, 1949. From the time that I can remember I was a hoodlum, what they call, you know, a bad teenager. 'Cause like, when I was twelve years old, we used to go around and take fruits from fruit stands, and eating apples. We'd go on the park and play around with girls, I liked to hang around with lots of girls. So like I never paid nobody no mind. I listen to my mother, you know, she tells me, "Come in the house before dark," you know, and all the other fellows be hanging it out, you know—parties, play records on the street corners, sitting in the gutter, watching the people come by. Whenever we would see a white man, you know, figure like this here, well, he rich; I'd better run away and hide because he might see that I'm very poor. I used to do things like that, I used to see

a white guy and sit way back in the train. I didn't realize, you know, what life was about until I was fourteen and I had a fight with a bunch of white guys in town. The guy told me—he's dead, he got shot and he's dead now—he told me, he says, "You go to our school and you're the only colored boy in our school, but yet you're out here and you're fighting. This don't make no sense." 'Cause, you see, the problem was that I was too thick-headed. I didn't pay nobody no mind. I just went along. Well, we stopped fighting and I started hanging around with them and then a couple of colored boys moved around the block and they start calling me "white." 'Cause I was friendly with the white boys from the school. Yeah, they call me "white." You know what I did? I told them, I said it like this, "Yeah, I might be white, but yet I'm getting this education."

You see, I always wanted, you know, to finish school. What you really need today, and I refer this to all black people period, is to stay in school and get an education. No matter how much people throw you out, they throw you out because they don't want you there or because your attendance is bad . . . I know why the attendance is bad for black people: 'cause they ain't got the clothing to wear, they ain't got the money to get to school. A lot of people walk for miles to go to school. So, I would advise all black people to stay in school and get their education—not just high school but even to go out further to college. If they could finish college, even keep trying to advance themselves, 'cause a college diploma is not the last step of school 'cause you could be taking school all your life, you know, like master degree and all of them.

The white people are afraid of the black

people rising up from the lowest form. They are afraid the black people are coming out of the ghettos and making something out of themselves and that's the main reason why President Kennedy and that guy Martin Luther King got killed, 'cause they was two people that I could at least say made some kind of progress towards the black people, to try and give them a way to come out of the ghettos and the slum areas and poverty and things like that. At least they gave them, you know, some kind of way.

Education is about the best thing for the black person; even the white person, they need education, too, the poor ones. The best way for a black person to make something is to come out and put whatever knowledge he got together and what the white man teach him, gain his knowledge and get above what he's teaching you. That's the best way for anybody to accomplish something.

I'm staying in school for a reason. 'Cause I feel I can help myself. I can help my younger brothers come up better than I was. I have to. The reason I have to is because I don't want them to feel that they are lacking. I want my younger brothers to go about life easier than I went by it. I mean decent clothes, I want them to have clothes, I mean decent clothes where you don't have to wear the same pants for three days. Or even getting up in the morning and they want to brush their teeth and they ain't got a toothbrush or toothpaste or they even got nothing to eat. I want them to get up, wake up, and have breakfast and things like that.

I wake up early in the morning and there ain't no heat in the wintertime. It's cold and we ain't got that many blankets to stay warm with, plus that the hot water

be cold, and you have to wash up in cold water or put water in a pot to heat it and wash your face to go to school. And then I'd be hungry, too. Mom ain't going to get up to make no breakfast or nothing, so I have to go on to school. I wanted to beat somebody in school for a toasted corn muffin. That was my favorite breakfast, a toasted corn muffin and a glass of water. That was my daily breakfast whenever I was fortunate enough to get a quarter or something.

Fortunately we got a toaster recently. The first toaster we ever had since I can remember, you know, that you toast bread with? My Aunt Maggie gave it to us. The demand for that toaster was a great thing and when we got the supply it was a great thing, you know what I mean? It was one of those wonderful days when you see something that you really need, a toaster. I was surprised. I didn't even know what it was. I mean I'd seen the box but I didn't read it. I had my mind on something else. Still, when I heard it was a toaster, I had to go and look at it myself. Had to toast with a slice of bread. Come to think of it, we had no bread that day either. I went next door to Davis' house and got a slice of bread and toasted it.

You want to know something funny? You might think it's funny but I think it's just me. I carry my toothbrush in my pocket every place. I go out and brush my teeth. When we go to basketball games, and run track, and I'm all sweaty, I go home and take my clothes and I go around to my cousin's house and take a shower. But during the week I take a bath at home, you know. I usually wind up taking a shower twice a week at my cousin's house, and take a bath once a week at my home. But when you get in

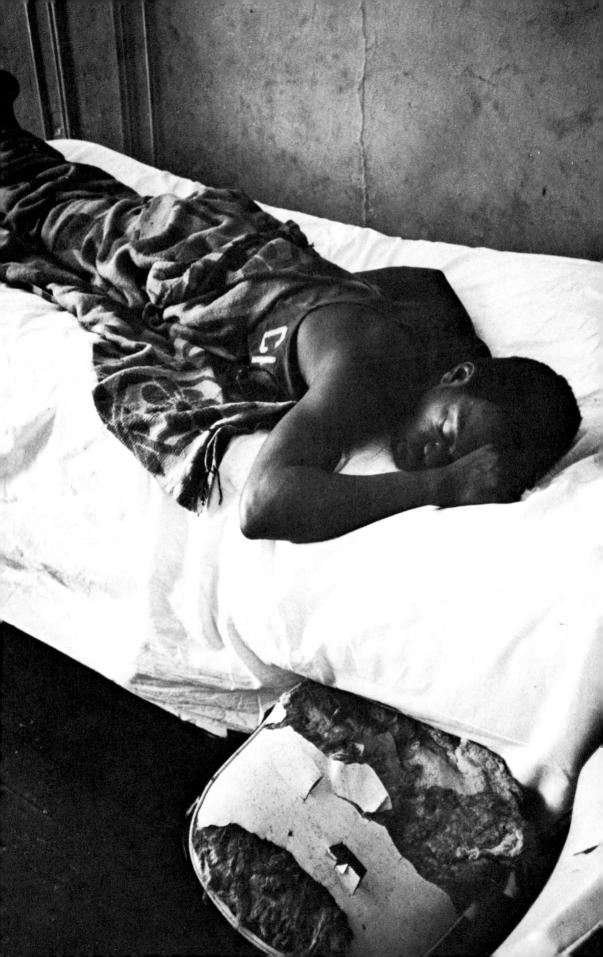

the tub and you wash yourself, you know like, when you're washing, the dirt comes right back on so you feel like, "I took a bath but I'm not clean."

I used to wash my socks every night, 'cause I had to wear them for months, the same pair of socks. I wash them the night before I go to school and when I come home from school I wash them again for the next day. One particular Monday that I didn't wash them that night, I washed them that morning. I put them in the oven to dry. I put in a pair of sneakers one day and the oven burned them up.

Clothes. That's my main problem. I don't care too much about anything but clothes, 'cause like if you have a lot of clothes it seems like you got everything you need. I used my track shirt as my undershirt. I used track shoes for sneakers to go around, and used the jacket to wear as a jacket, 'cause like I have to have a jacket at certain times. I ain't got no clothes. I mean there's a lot of times I went to school with a hole in my shoe, but yet I didn't quit. I feel sorry for the people that are too lazy to help themselves. Not just the colored, the white too.

You know, it's kind of hard for a person to believe that, as poor as I am, I never stole nothing but oranges and apples and things like that. See, I used to work in a food store when I was ten, twelve. I cut it out, man, you know why? 'Cause he's a white guy, he was using me as a slave, man. He used to pay the white boy thirty or forty dollars a week and he would give me ten dollars. I mean, after all, they did the same thing I did. We cleaned out the vegetable stand. I used to work on Saturdays and he used to give me ten dollars, something like I was too young to receive a higher pay because I had no working papers. So, I told him I wasn't

even supposed to be working there. He is supposed to be giving me more than that. And he'd give the other guys twenty to thirty dollars a week and they wasn't sixteen either. You know what happened to him? He went out of business.

It's hard growing up here. There aren't many kids around the block, young boys around sixteen, seventeen years old. I betcha you couldn't go around there and find more than ten. I bet you the majority of them are in jail. For instance, there was a guy, a good friend of mine, Eddie Johnson. He got so involved with the people that he got busted for homicide for the older man, Manuel Lopez. Got busted for homicide. Then this guy Harris that was with him. And then there's other guys that got busted for burglaries, manslaughter, possession of dope, narcotics. Frank Williams, for instance. Rat. Rat? You know, Rat and Pop? That's the nickname we give him, Rat and Pop, but his name is Frank Williams, and some other guy were dealing dope, which I don't know if they was dealing dope or not, but they got busted for dope, saying they had possession of dope in their pocket. And the people that gave them that dope, I betcha they still out there on the street and there are young boys going to jail for it, trying to make a way, trying to get some clothes on their back, trying to get food in their house. They figure they go for a job, people don't want to hire them, but yet they got to come out here and they hustle. They start dealing dope, and the next thing they know, they in jail.

They have to make it for themselves 'cause most of them don't have fathers. My father, he died sometime after World War II, so I didn't know him too good. I remember he looked like my brother Paul, he looks just like him. I miss him 'cause like a lot of times when you have problems like, well, like I used to always have problems for many reasons, you know, money problems. So you say, well, this guy got a father, he's always had a father, he's always, you know, appealing to his father for help. But like a lot of times I could be sitting down and I'd be thinking, "Wonder if I had a father how life would be so easy." 'Cause like in school the first thing they ask me is, "Tell your father to come in to school" and I feel kind of bad 'cause they know my father is dead and they keep bringing it up. It's a lonely feeling 'cause a lot of times you want to lean on somebody; you need somebody that could try and talk to you and tell you certain things. The problems that I have I can't, you know, express them to my mother 'cause a lot of times she don't understand it.

My mother is a remarkable woman. You know how she got an education? She didn't finish high school. My mother got an education off the subway trains. She'd look at words on the train and write them down and she come home and say, "I learned a new word today," and she would spell it out. She's been doing that for years. She can read. She can write. She reads better than I do. She went to school up until the eighth grade. She was thirteen when she had her first baby, she was in the eighth grade. This was down South. My mother, she had it worse than I had. She used to go out in the fields and pick cotton. My mother used to work all the time, before Paul was born, when she was small. They had to pick a hundred pounds of cotton for fifty cents or something like that. They would pick beans and potatoes. My mother, she used to run in potato sack races and a lot of other things. She was pretty good. And all this time still a poor family but yet still happy. We manage.

Like we have no finance to get enough bulbs to go all over the house, so what you have you have to make the best use of it. So you figure if you have a light in the bedroom and nobody is using it you just transcript the bulb to another socket, is really 'cause we don't have enough money to buy enough light bulbs to go all over the house. There is a lot of problems even with blankets at night when it's cold in the wintertime. But I'm used to these things, so it ain't no big thing. If I get a new blanket I feel like, "Wow, man, I got me another luxury," you know. Like to other people they use them to throw them on the floor for babies to play on and what not, but I need them to keep me warm 'cause a lot of times it is so cold and the super don't send up no steam anyway.

And then we use those pie pans which are from my mother's job. She works at Chock Full O' Nuts on 34th Street. She brings pie home once in a while, so we use the pans to eat out of because there aren't enough plates. There ain't enough silverware, plates, glasses, pots to cook in. You have to use your head, you know what I mean? You have to make efforts.

See, Geneva, my sister, she's a remarkable young lady, 'cause she had two kids but yet, you know, she dropped out of school but wrote to the home study program. Wrote to the home study program for lessons at home and she been taking these lessons for a long time now. I'm pretty sure she's going to get a high school equivalency diploma and plus when she goes back to school she's going to get a regular high school diploma. Now, not many girls would do this. Right? You tell me how many girls you know

131

that had kids and quit school and are still trying to get a diploma; now that's something else. Plus she was even working a little while in the hospital as a nurse's aide, and she had to quit 'cause, you know, the stomach was showing or something like that.

Everybody always saying, well, I know what it is to be like you. I know how it feels when you go someplace, and they say, "Well, you can't come in here because you're black," or, "You can't come in here because you're white." The color and shit, that ain't nothing, man. It depends on the man. Me, as a black man, I respect myself to the highest. Even with the things that I lack—like clothing, food now and then, money to go to school, even a job or education—I want to advance myself forward. Even with all these handicaps and mainly my color—my black race, period—at least I'm not stealing. I'm poor, period. Even if you're poor there is a way that you could try and get up. Only way a poor person going to be able to get anyplace is if he help himself; he can never depend on nobody to lend him nothing. When I want something I go out and get it. I don't go around stealing it. Like if I have fifty cents or something I play a game of pool for a quarter, and then I quit the pool and go around the block and say, "Hey, man, why don't you make a good investment—lend me a half and you get a dollar back." So most likely you catch one of those fools out there—not exactly fools, you say; well, people that think their heart is together, you know, like they want to show like a reflection towards you, like a feeling towards you—so they lend me the half and during the time they are thinking of getting their profit. So after that you continue hustling until you make enough

money. I must owe my school about fifteen million dollars, the people in that school. It seems like every day go by there's somebody I beat for a dime. "Yea, brother, lend me a dime until tomorrow." He lends me a dime.

It's good being on top. Going to track meets and things like that. It's a good feeling when you win and you see all the girls look at you and everybody look at you and congratulate you, but it's a bad feeling when you lose. Dig that. I got disappointed at one meet. I think I lost. It was the New York Rally. I didn't exactly lose, my rally team lost. That was the hurting day of my life 'cause my school lost a new meet record for the first time, that we'd been practicing that rally together for three years, that same rally team. That was the first time we had a meet record and blew it. I'll never forget that.

The main reason I want to go to college is because I want to be an "All-American." Unless I get to college, I can't do it. I can't do it in high school. I don't want to feel that I went to school for twelve years and I have to work for a dollar. I don't want somebody to boss me, 'cause I'm my own boss.

I had kind of a dream once about that. This particular day I was laying down and it seemed like I was . . . it's hard to say, there was like a glow, you know, and it was telling me . . . like my mother was saying like, "Make it, 'cause this is your life." That's all. It just came out just like that in my mind, like the room was light. You know, the actual light of the wall—see, like it came to my mind to say this. Ever since then I never gave it up. I always did it. And like every year it seems like I improve in my ability with different sports. I went all around. I played

baseball all year around. Like I always play, even with a stickball bat. The first thing I think of is baseball. I've been playing baseball ever since I was nine years old. The day I really became a runner I was in the park and a policeman was chasing us 'cause we stole some oranges and ever since then I love to run. I got away, but my mother made me give them back. She beat me and I gave them back. I didn't steal nothing since then except lunches. Me and Lopez, we go down to lunch, 'cause I'm in the lunch service squad, so we get there around 11:40, we go in there and we say, "One guy snuck in, better write down his name"; and they'd be writing down his name and we'd pick some pickles and sandwiches and then we go outside, come back in and take our posts, and then we get our lunch.

I'm always low on money, you know. Like my mother gave me the money to rent the tuxedo, fifteen dollars and seventy-five cents, for the high school prom. I put ten dollars on a tuxedo, so that means I have $5.75 left. So, I figure, well, as long as I got to get a corsage, so I asked my man, I says, "Hey brother, you know, man, I'm going to my prom tomorrow." He says, "So what, see me tomorrow and I'll give you some money." You know, like this guy Tommy or this man working in the liquor store or something like that. I call him Minnesota Fats, 'cause he's fat and got a bald head. So I told him, I said, "I'm going to my prom tomorrow; you might as well give me a graduation present." He said, "Well, see me tomorrow." So I ran into him the day I was supposed to go to the prom (I didn't go to school 'cause I'm trying to figure how to get some money), so I ran into him and I said, "I don't need no money

for the prom, man." He said, "What you going to do!" I said, "I just want two dollars and seventy-five cents for a corsage." So then he says, "No, I don't give it to you. I ain't got no two dollars." So I said, "I'll take what you got." So he gave me a dollar. So this other guy came long and he said, "You're graduating?" I said, "Yeah, why don't you help me get on, get down and get my corsage. I got to get my woman a corsage." He said, "How much is it?" I said, "$2.75." He said, "Oh, here's a dollar for graduation. That's the best I can do." Now I had two dollars. So then I went to the whiskey store and I told the boss, "Hey brother, I need some money, man, for the prom. When I get some I'll pay you back." So I took the $2.75 with the five dollars and I was walking to get the corsage and I see these guys shooting dice. So I went on along and start shooting and ended up with thirty-seven dollars and fifty cents. I bought me a pair of shoes for twenty-two dollars—twenty dollars and ninety-eight cents, rather—patent leather, dig that. So, I bought a corsage and I had exactly six dollars and twenty-seven cents 'cause with the twenty cents I bought a hamburger and with the seven cents I bought some crystal mints. It's a candy.

So I then went up. I put the corsage in my refrigerator and I came down. I had on a pair of old brown pants that I wore all week long, so then I went downstairs and my boy, Minnesota Fats, that works in the whiskey place, calls me and he says, "Come here, my man." I said, "What you want?" Bang, he threw me a ten spot, you know. He gave me a ten spot. He gave me ten dollars. Next thing I knew, somebody else came up and gave me another ten dollars. The people from the stores and things know me, I guess. I guess they're just giving a graduation present. So Minnesota gave me ten and this other lady gave me ten and my girlfriend's father gave me five dollars. That means I had twenty-five dollars. So I had twenty-five dollars and then this guy that I used to hang around with, this Spanish boy, his name was Billy, so he gave me $2.50 and I had $27.50 and next thing I knew I was shooting dice. I started shooting dice again on the corner. This is the same day of the prom. So I start gambling. And that's when I went in my slide and I said "Wow!" I looked in my pocket and I seen so much dough, you know, I winded up—I think I had sixty-five dollars that night. Man, what a night!

It was a feeling like I can't even explain the feeling, it was so good. Oh, wow, I felt like I was the President or somebody. I had me a chauffeur, had me a car—I didn't even have a car with me—I just felt like I owned the world. I felt like I was a king, another Nat King Cole. Everybody said I looked like him. Yeah, they call me young Nat. I killed them though, they couldn't say nothing to me. You know, I was dancing and nobody could dance as good as I could.

I was the only Negro boy at the prom—rather, I'm not saying Negro—I was the only black man at the prom and my woman was the only black girl. We got at least two hundred black boys in my school; at least fifty graduates that are black, and none of them showed up to the prom. The main reason, I figured, maybe they didn't have no money. Anyway, this was just me and myself and my woman and everybody else, they're just out there to be out there, but I'm out there to enjoy myself. I mean, to really bring out what it would be like if I was rich or something like that, or just being a wealthy person for one night or being clean enough to know that the white man ain't no better than I am, to even prove it to him this particular night. The attention I got was outrageous, really; even the white people looked at me and said I looked good. They didn't say, "Well, boy, go back where you came from," or "Black boy, go on back down your block, we don't want you up here." They didn't say that this time. They say, "Come on in, dance with the young girls. Have a ball." Yeah, but when you ain't got no bucks you're up tight; they call you, "Hey doggie, go on back down there." You know that famous record colored people sing. I'm saying colored people because they're ignorant when they do that. "We shall overcome." The white man made that record for a reason. When he says, "We shall overcome," that means he wants to overcome the black people, which he hasn't done it. And when he say "we," he speaking of the white people behind him is going to overcome the other colored people that are coming up.

I was killing them, boy. I was class. Anybody that looked at me, I knew I was clean. I was so clean that I felt like I was a millionaire, boy. And I had a few bucks in my pocket. We was going to the Copacabana, but when we got there it was all fulled up, after reservations and everything. So then we went on to Small's Paradise. This was my night and no matter how much the white man tried to bring me down or another black man tried to influence me, this is one day that John Smith in himself is out there and he's out there to represent himself as a black person with enough money or decent clothing to compare with anybody else out there. This was the most important

night in my life. That's why I tried to make the best of it. Oh, when I went to sleep that day and woke up I didn't want to take the tuxedo off. When I took it off it seemed that it just drifted, but I can't never forget it though; I'll never forget it as long as I live. The High School Prom.

That particular night will be a night for me and definitely my woman, my girl-friend rather, Suwon, to remember. I know that was the first time she ever was in a gown and went to such formal places, like the Park Terrace, a respectable hotel. She looked fine, you know?

I went with Suwon 'cause after I got started seeing her I got the impression that she thought she was cute, you know. And I like her, though, because she was the type of person that she carried herself in a way of respect, you know, for her person. You understand what I mean? A lot of young girls they see you, they say, "Hey baby, what's happening?" you know, "How you doing? How's your woman?" But Suwon was a different type of person. She says, "Well, how you doing?" "How's your girlfriend?" I said, "All right." She says, "Oh, I'll see you later." You know. I said, "All right." So it was that thing. Then one day we were all standing by the train and Suwon was there with Rosalind and me and my sister. And I looked at Suwon and, you know, like I had a dime and I dropped it and she bent down to pick it up. So as she bent down to pick up the dime she handed it to me. I said thanks. The min-ute I grabbed the hand, you know, took hold of the hand, it's just that I didn't want to let it go. I said, "You know, you're looking mighty sweet to be so young, you know." She said, "Well, you're not so old yourself, mister." Like that. So. I says, "Where you going now? Is it all

right if I hang around?" She says, "I don't know." Like that. I said, "Well, later." And I left. So the next day she was in my house. She kept coming up my house.

Then one day we was walking down the block and I ran into her and she says —'cause I had a lollypop or something . . . I was sucking a lollypop for some reason—"You want me to buy you a bigger sucker?" I said, "What are you calling me a sucker, on the sly?" She says, "No." I said, "All right, you can buy me a lollypop." You know, I was just doing it for the fun of it. To see what she would do. You know. She bought the lollypop. And then we start talking. You know, I said, "Well, look, why don't we try and get together? Maybe I can take you out sometime." She said, "Naw, I wouldn't like that." "Well, that's your business." You know. So I left. And then we was by the train again and she was up there and Rosalind was arguing, you know, they was having an argument. So I said, "Suwon, can I speak to you for a minute?" She said, "Yeah." I said, "Look." I said, "Look, let me stop kidding myself." I said, "Look, I dig you. You all right, you know." I said, "Uh, who you going with?" She said, "Well, I was wondering how long it was going to take you to ask me, you know." I said, "What you mean? I didn't even know you had any ideas about it." She says, "Uh," like that, she didn't say nothing . . . the next thing I knew I was going with her.

I wouldn't say she's my whole life. I mean, she's a great part of my life. My life is what I make it, you know. 'Cause like I want to be a star, man. I want to be recognized by the public. But not by a public where they can say, well, this dude is a con man. You know. I want to be something like maybe another Jesse

Owens, or Bob Hayes, or Bill Russell or somebody like that. I could do it if I get a break, which I need one, you dig it.

Well, I got one thing. I got my diploma, my high school diploma. It was a real good feeling to see yourself walking in front of a stage to receive your diploma and all the people looking at you, and your mother there waiting for the big day, and you go up and you receive your diploma. The way I felt about it, I felt I finally made it. I said, "God bless me," and let me get out of here, 'cause it was so hot and I was already getting wet. What a day. I went to my mother's job. I was looking for my mother. I usually see her with a blue waitress uniform so I saw her and I didn't even recognize her; she looked like she owned the joint and I said, "Wow, what is this? Where is your uniform?" I thought she had on such a nice dress to come to the graduation, so then another girl that works there said, "You didn't hear the news? Today your mother got raised as assistant manager of Chock Full O' Nuts." I almost fell off my chair 'cause it was hard to believe, so I had to ask the manager herself. "Is this true? Is she a boss now?" And I said to myself, "Wow, they finally got a black boss in Chock Full O' Nuts!" I felt that she deserved it. It's a remarkable thing how one good turn deserves another.

Pretty soon after that, you know, that's when Suwon got pregnant. I knew she was pregnant but I didn't . . . I knew it before she knew it really, I think. Anyway she told me, she said, "John, uh," she said, "I think I'm pregnant." I said, "Well, go to the doctor and get a checkup." So she went to the doctor. She told her mother that she was going to the dentist or something. So she went to the doctor and she got a checkup and she said,

"Yeah. I'm pregnant, you know." So she said, "What you want to do? You want me to get rid of it?" I said, "What?" You know, she asked me if she should get rid of it. I says, "Suwon, look. If you really care for me." You know. 'Cause at that time we started liking each other a lot. We done a lot of different things together. I said, "I'd never want you to get rid of nothing that's mine." And, "I'm pretty sure it's mine because I know you ain't been around anybody else."

I said, "I want to marry you because you love me and I love you and forget about the kid at the present time, you know, something could happen that . . . I don't ever want you to feel we got married because of the kid, I want to get married because you love me." I said, "Then we raise our kid." And then she looked at me and she grabbed me and kissed me.

You know, I wouldn't want nobody, no other man taking my responsibilities on. You know, like my child. I wouldn't want no man to have to support my kid, nor nothing like that. And that's not the main reason, the main reason, you know, since I been around Suwon for a while, I grown, you know, fond of her, and I could see, man, what type . . . she's a decent woman, man, you know? And I . . . like I explain things to her. Like I say, it takes a good woman to make a good man. And she's got something I could depend on, man. You know . . . faithful . . . you could trust. You could like compare with other people. That can understand problems, mistakes; they know how to go about building a home, how to, uh, make their man pleased, happy. Things like that. And all this fits in, you know.

"The way I feel about it," I said, "you love a person, you willing to help this person; you willing to take this person's pains; you willing to sacrifice for this person; you're willing to understand them. It's really to build an image of this person within yourself." That's my definition of love. And to know the emotion of being around them or not around them . . . how do you feel . . . It's the feeling of them, you know, it's really to understand what it is with the person which makes you so close to them. You have to be, in other words, a part of them. You got to be part of the person. Not just say, "Well, I love you," and when you go home, uh, the next dude that come along, why baby, like you know, he kiss me sweet and everything, damn, he kiss better than John, so I love him. That doesn't mean nothing, man. What I feel about it is, actually, getting to understand a person's emotions, the way he feels, not just him, the way you feel toward him, what you could gain by being with him . . . how to communicate with him . . . how to take his problems and your problems and build off them instead of them breaking both of you on down.

Then I told her, I said, "Another thing the matter, like if I don't . . . like if you found a man that you want because you're young, say you're young and there's going to be plenty of fellows that dig you. Right. Say that you find a fellow that you want. No matter how much you say you love me don't ever take no pity upon nobody." I said, "If you come out and tell a person the truth it won't hurt them as much as it would if you hide it from him and he finds out." I said, "Suwon, if I ever, which I doubt, find a woman that I think I would care more for, that I could build, you know, a better life with . . . I think I . . . I wouldn't hesitate to say, 'Well, Suwon, we can't make

it, you know.' " When I come I don't want you to have to tell me, "Well, my man is here. You can't come now." We let this man know that your ex-boyfriend —or your ex-husband or whatever the case may be—had a chile here and he's coming to see his chile. And there's nothing between me and you, or if it is just tell him, "Well, look, this is his chile and if you can't cope with my husband coming to see his chile we can't make it."

I care about the baby because I'm a man. It's really my mother's fault, because she said to me, "John, if you got something that's yours and you know it's yours, build with it. Don't ever slight nothing that's yours." I've got responsibility now. You know. So I said to myself: Right now, tomorrow, I'm going to take a test for the New York City University, and after that I'm going out looking for a job. The reason I'm getting a job is to get money for clothes and things to wear to college and money to help my family. You know, like when I go to school in the fall I'd probably be working at school, and then I'd be playing ball and I hope I can make a future of basketball or baseball or some field of sports which I participate in. My one goal is to become an All-American and I'm pretty sure I'm capable of doing it if I get the break; if I get the chance to go to college I know I can do it.

I got to move. So I went down to Southern Boulevard—the New York State Employment Agency—in the Bronx. I walked in there and I told them that I wanted to fill out an application for employment. So the lady said, "Well, how long are you willing to wait for a job?" And I told her that I wanted a job without being in a training program. She said it takes about six months. Then I

142

explained to her my girl was having a baby and I need a job right away. So she assigned me to another lady, named Miss Green, in the same building. So I went to see Miss Green and Miss Green assigned me to a lady at the Information Desk, and then I filled out another application for employment, and they assigned me to the United Housing Foundation downtown. I talked to the boss at the United Housing Foundation, but he was only offering seventy-two dollars, you know. And I told him that I was a high school graduate and I told him that that wasn't enough money. He wanted me to pick up the mail in the morning. Be like an office clerk—working with the typewriter, printing up address plates. So that's all. I mean, it's not a hard job. It's from nine to five and you get some good meals. It only costs a dollar and you eat as much as you want.

I told him that the reason I wasn't too sure if I wanted the job was because they weren't paying enough money, and plus I was looking for a job with a future. I don't want to work where I can see I wasn't going to make no kind of progress or build myself up with no kind of background or nothing. So he guaranteed me in three months, if I was still working there—being to work on time and doing my work—that he would give me a raise and in about a year, he said, that I should advance myself up to, you know, a regular operator on a machine by myself, without any help, and that I might be able to train somebody else.

He just looked at me and he said, "Well, this is a big organization and people get promoted every day. It's up to you, Mr. Smith," that's what he said, "how well you advance yourself in the organization. You've got a good oppor-

tunity because you're young." And he said, "When I graduated from college I worked as an office clerk." He said, "Don't feel so bad because like in a year or maybe two years, how do you know? You might be a foreman on a machine, or something like that." And I said, "Well, I'm going to work on it and I'll do my best and I'll see what I can do." And I told him, "If you don't happen to give me a raise and I find a better job, with a better type of future, I will quit."

Then I got fired 'cause Joey in the office didn't want me to take his girl, 'cause his girl kept telling me, "Wow! You dress nice." And I'd look at her, and I'd say, "Yeah, baby. An everyday thing." And he gets mad, and goes tells a lot of lies behind my back. He went and told the boss that I'm high and I'm this here. And I never been high a day on that job.

I got me another job though. I went to some more of those employment agencies and I'm doing my work, minding my business. I have nothing to do and this Chinese guy that work there—Charley Chan, I call him—the lady asks him, "Give him something to do, Mr. (whatever his name is—I call him Chan)," and he gave me some papers to sort. So I was sorting the papers and they call me in there. You know, the boss, whatever his name is. He says, "John, come here a minute." So I go inside. I say, "Yes, suh," just like that. I sit down, and this broad and Mr. Chan were there. So Mr. Chan and the broad leave. Rather, Mr. Chan leaves, and the broad stay there. And he says, "John, Miss (whatever her name is—I can't remember the broad's name), she says you're not doing your work fast enough, and we need a man who can respond to catch on real fast. You know, be able to keep our business going.

143

'Cause this is a big organization, and when we fall down, like one mistake go wrong, the whole organization go down." I looked at him, and I told him, "Yes, sir." He said, "How do you feel about it?" I said, "Mister, I been doing my work faster than she's doing hers. How come you think I asked her for more work to do?" And he looks at me and he says, "She don't think so." Like that. She says, "You made a mistake on a file card." I said, "Yeah. I did. But I was man enough to correct my own mistakes. You don't have to correct it for me." Like that, you know.

So then he says, "Well, I can't no longer use you because you're not working rapidly enough." I looked at him and I say, "Yeah. I'm not working rapidly enough, and I make mistakes, right?" I said, "I know one thing, at least, to my understanding and knowledge of myself, that I been doing your work right and everything, and doing fast enough. How come you think she got me sorting out the papers now? 'Cause she ain't got nothing for me to do."

He says, "Well, uh, I'm going to have to let you go."

If he's wrong, tell the man he's wrong where he can make a right way. Not wait till you feel that being as I'm the boss, and the man is wrong, I don't know he's wrong, 'cause I'm only listening to what some other person tell me, and I'm going to fire him like that. He don't know, boy, pride is a hurting thing, Jack. When you hurt a man's pride, you hurting yourself. You dig it? That's bad business. That goes to show you, no matter how hard you try to please the whitey, you can't please him. Unless you shining his shoes. I bet you if I was shining somebody's shoes, or was down in a mail room, or

something like that, or mopping their floors, I wouldn't have got fired. They'd say, "Yeah! He's a good worker." He sweat his ass off, that's why he's a good worker. I could tell the dog to bend over when I want to.

I'm tired of the white man putting his bullshit over me, that's what it is. That's just where it's at. It's not because I'm black. I'm proud I'm black. If a man said, "Look, I'll give you anything in the world to be white," I'd beat his ass. I couldn't be white for nobody, 'cause a white man ain't shit. Unless he's a good man. And you run into some good men. A man that feels like he's a man, not because he's white, because he's a man. And that's a man. You don't find very many men. And black people are the same way. Some of them ain't shit, because they let the whitey go build on them. You see a black man now, swearing he's white 'cause he got a Cadillac and some money. And he don't want to say nothing to the dogs out there begging. I walk down the street every day. If I got fifty cents in my pocket, and I see a bum—I don't care if he's white or black—and he say, "Mister, you got a dime for a cup of coffee?" I give it to him.

I had *the* job. The job was easy. It was ridiculous! I couldn't even call it a job, 'cause it was nice, you know, it **was** respectable. You got to come neat, in a tie and whatnot. A respectable place. I never thought the people would come out like they did. Just when I was beginning to like it, too. That's why a lot of brothers are out on the street now, stinging, robbing people, mugging, 'cause when they get a job, man, they be doing their best, and the white man get jealous 'cause he feels this man could do better than he doing. "I got to get rid of him!" So they fire him, so a man, he lose his

pride. He seen that he put all his effort in it, you know. They give you something, and then they take it away from you. Just like when a black man, he builds up a store, and the government comes along and hit him with taxes, so they can take his land away.

And people tell you jobs are open for everybody on the street. There's no reason for you to be stealing. That's a lie! If you're a thief, I'd advise you to be a good thief. 'Cause you working, Jim, you ain't going to succeed unless you got some kind of influence. 'Cause in two jobs I had, I don't see why in the world I got fired.

There's another problem in my life, you know. I been going to court for more than a year and a half, and one time I had to go a whole week straight. You know, it was ready and the judge never showed up. The reason for going to court was I was accused of starting a fire to a shoeshine parlor at 502 East 174th Street and Third Avenue.

I would go there during the week, to shoot pool and rap to the young girls, like that I was hanging out with. It was a social club, like. I could shoot pool, and like after I got on the street patrol of the Morrisania Community Corporation the main reason for me being there was trying to find out about these dope dealers that was hanging out in there, drug addicts, you know, users of drugs. I think I was accused because the owner would lose business from the people that were coming in there to buy dope, see, and then they would buy beer to hang out to wait on the dope pushers and whatnot. I figure he must have felt I was trying to slow down his business or something. Plus that, he knew that I knew his wife and I knew some of his girlfriends.

I figure maybe that's one of the reasons there.

Well, see, the particular night of the fire, I came out of my house and I was supposed to meet this girl named Pat, so I walked down toward the bar to meet this girl. I knocked on her door and her mother says she's down by the bar, so I went down by the bar, and I ran into this crap game, so I started shooting dice. I had a dollar and some change. I won $85.75. So like I asked the man if he had fifty cents left. He said, "Won't you shoot the fifty cents, man, give me a play and let me try and get my money back?" So I said, "All right, it's a bet." Like that. You know, at first I was saying to myself, "Why should I gamble my eighty-five dollars to give this man this fifty-cent play?" So I gave it to him, and I won, so I bent down to pick up the fifty cents, and it was about six or seven men standing around us. So as I bend down to pick up the fifty cents, these three men jumped on me. When they pushed me down, then this other guy, he jumped on me and the other guy, and they was snatching the money from me. So they took the money, and they ran up toward Third Avenue. And I see one run into Lonnie Melvin's shoeshine parlor. So I went in there after him.

I just walked in, so I seen this guy standing in the corner, so I asked him, "Didn't you just take me off?" He says, "Take you off?" He says, "Nah, I didn't take you off!" Man, like that. So I didn't say nothing, you know. Then he got all nasty, start cursing and shit. So I turned around and went to walk out and then he grabbed me and put this knife at my throat. And that's when these three Spanish boys that were shooting pool, they pull out this gun and told him to get his hands off of me. So when he let me go I was scared. So I went to the phone booth, there was this phone like. I call the policeman. And the patrol car came and when it came, you know, he was looking to see who called, so I went over to the patrol car, and I told him I had just won some money shooting dice, and people just robbed my money, and I wanted to get my money back. So the dude, the cop, said, "Don't you know that, uh, you could get yourself in trouble by gambling," you know, illegal gambling. He said, "Why don't you be a good boy and go on home?" So when I walked up toward Third Avenue, the patrol car followed me, then I went on home. I was crying and all, you know. As far as I was concerned, that was the end of the whole night. The place was suppose to have burnt down that Sunday evening.

About two and a half weeks later I was arrested. They have on record nine days. But it was longer than that. When I was arrested, I was taken to the 48th Precinct. I stayed in the bullpen overnight. I went to night court. They charged me with arson in the first degree. And then from there they sent me to Brooklyn House of Detention, where they took my footprints, my handprints, and all sorts of prints—pictures. I stayed in Brooklyn for about two weeks. Then like my mother bailed me out.

They offered me twice—was it two or four times?—to cop out to a misdemeanor felony and for three years' parole, you know, probation. But that's not a guaranteed probation. That's like, he said, I would make sure I would be on the street. So, but I feel this way, if I'm not guilty I wasted all this time—if I was guilty I would have copped out before and got the parole. Why should I cop out now,

right just at the end of my trial?

If I cop out to a misdemeanor this is the situation. I could get a Class D Misdemeanor, that's one to three years parole, or I could get one to three years in jail. It depends on what the judge wants to give me. The D.A. is trying to get the conviction real quick, you see. They figure if I cop out now, there's the conviction, saying that I did. 'Cause if you cop out, you got to actually say you did everything they said you did, which I didn't, so I'm not copping out if they offered me twenty years parole, you know. So I'll just go on, but if I blow trial, then it might come down to . . . the judge might throw the book at me—that's twenty-five years maximum. Or I could get one to four years in a reformatory school. And then I got a chance there of parole, too. So like either way it goes, man, I still got the chance of parole, and I still got the chance of going to jail, so I might as well wait for the jury's verdict. I went this far, right?

It's bad, though, you know. I couldn't get no witnesses 'cause they're scared to testify. This neighborhood ain't shit. They trying to screw you up every time they get you. If you're nice, or you're a respectable person, if you never did nothing, they try and throw you in little corners. "Come on, man, let's do this here. Let's do that." You say, "No, man. I ain't got no heart." "You know, you a faggot." You this, you that. But you going to have to take a lot of that, Jimmy, if you don't want to go to jail, boy.

I talked to Suwon about all this. I said, "Well, look. If I get three years in jail, or four years, would you wait?" She said, "Yes." I said, "Well, what security do I have?" She said, "The only thing you have is my word." And then she grabbed me and kissed me. She said, "I hope it's

good enough for you, 'cause I would wait." So that's why it gave me courage to go on with the trial, you know.

So after all that, I went to court again. They couldn't find no verdict. So then my lawyer went in the chambers with the judge and the D.A. and stayed in there for about a half an hour. Told me to wait for him. I laid outside. So he came back and he say, "John, before I didn't tell you to cop out or nothing." He say, "I didn't tell you to cop . . . I let you make your own decision, but I'm your lawyer, and being as I understand the situation the way the jury felt, and the way the judge feel and everything, I'm telling you to cop out now to—" And I say, "What?" He says, "Unlawfully being on the property. That's a thirty-day rap." You know. Thirty days. So in other words I get the thirty days or the judge is going to throw it out of court. Yeah, and that's the way it ended after a year—almost two years. A year and nine months. Imagine that.

Could have had three babies by then. You know, I had a dream about being married to Suwon last night. It was real hot. We got married, we went to the beach, you know. I was so happy. I felt like I was shooting fifty points a game in a basketball game. I felt like I ran an eight-second hundred-yard dash. I felt like I was a lawyer in the Supreme Court movement. Seemed like all my problems came back and instead of me being the victim I was the prosecutor. And I was defending the defendant, I was the lawyer. I was the star, instead of being the young man out there breaking his leg trying to be the star. I was high scorer instead of being the man that's trying to catch up. I was so high—happy, you know—and the next day I went and bought Suwon a baby crib and bassinet. She wanted that.

I don't know how I did it.

You know there's a card game every week by different people around my neighborhood. That's their stick. You know, hustling up money for the rent and food and whatnot. So, I went down—my mother was going to this ladies' card game, a party, a house party, they call it a social party. But they have a poker game. I went there and my mother was there and she knows I play poker fairly well. Like I told her, I said, "I want you to loan me ten dollars." She had twenty dollars. She said, "This all the money I got." So she gave me ten. So it was a ten-dollar table stake. That means you need ten dollars to sit down at the table. So, I got the ten dollars to sit down, and I started dealing the cards and I kept betting and getting aces and kings and whatnot and the next thing I end up with thirty, forty dollars. So, then I had about fifty dollars. I quit. I went to this other lady's house. I give my mother her ten dollars back, and I think ten dollars more or something like that. So, and I went to this other lady's house up around 177th Street, Third Avenue. See, they always give me invitations because they know I'm a pretty nice hustler, you know. I'm the only young boy around there that they would give invitations to because they know if I win, you know, no confusion; if I have money and I lose it, I never say much. I played and went home. I started counting. 'Cause I didn't realize how much money I had. I start counting. Oh, wow! Man! A hundred and five dollars. God. So I went, like I went to sleep.

So the next day I say, well, first thing I'm going to do is pay out Suwon's crib and basket—you know, bassinet. Claremont Parkway and 172nd to this place that has bassinets. It cost about sixteen dollars. With the wheels, and you can fold it up and carry it. So I paid something like $15.95. And I left there. I was looking for a baby crib. So I couldn't find any crib, so I went down to 16th Street, Park Avenue, and I paid on a baby crib. I put down twenty-five. I had put down twenty, and then I gave the dude five more one day. And with the crib and the bassinet together I owe about ten dollars.

I'm just going to let them deliver it and ring the bell and say, "Suwon Jones, sign for this." If you have to sign for it. "Who's it from?" "John Smith." Or, you know, whatever the case may be. And I come down Tuesday and maybe she say, "Thank you," and maybe she say, "Well, what the hell is this," you know. Just depends.

When I hold my new baby it's going to be an exciting moment. If I ever get the chance to hold it when it's newborn. I often think about it. I want it to be like me, you know. Try and get it to. I don't know, man. I can teach him the things that are out there, see, that I already experienced. Not in just saying, "Well, look baby, there's grief in this reefer. You're not supposed to smoke it," you know, " 'cause it's bad for you." And don't do this here and don't do that. I mean it might sound stupid. But, you know, like I'm a young man, but I figure this way: my son, when he's fifteen, sixteen years old, I got to expect him to be drinking, you know, smoking, maybe. Like if he's 'round the wrong people maybe he'll be using dope. But I'll never go out and say, "Well, you not my son, because you use dope." I will say, "Well look, man, now, like don't you dig yourself? I know what's happening, I been out here. I'm not going to tell you if you stop using dope you be a better person, 'cause you might even be worse, you might just don't care about

nothing. It's only, dope is nothing to play with. It's not the thing. You dig it?" You know, I explain it to him. Show him the problems with it. I actually show him, man. I'm not going to just *say* you can't . . . you can't tell a person something. When you tell a person it's like saying, well, listen to me now and forget it later. You have to actually show them. If you really want them to understand, you have to show them.

I can say, "Well look, son, if you going for a job, like always think in your mind of this here: not all the people in the world are prejudiced; if you got the ability to do it you can do it. It don't matter if you get turned down one place, don't give up, you know. There's other places for jobs, and education, and all these different fields and whatnot."

See, like I went through *hell*—a lot of things—you know, and I didn't have no father to tell me, so therefore, like the things I did, the things I seen and whatnot, it's not my mother's fault. She couldn't help it. It's because I was there, you know. And there wasn't no way of me escaping it, 'cause it was the only thing around me. Junkies. Dope addicts. Thieves. You know. All different type things. Whores. Prostitutes. Well, this is where it was at, you know. So I had to live with this, but I was man enough to live with this where I could learn different things about these people.

I feel this way. When my son—or my daughter, whatever—you know, when I have a chile, he won't have to go through this, you know what I'm saying? She won't have to say, well, damn, how am I going to get me a pair of shoes this week. Like where'm I going to get my next meal from, or I wonder if I can go to this school, if they allow Negroes at this school. Or if black men are allowed to go in this restaurant—you know, like down South? They have these signs, they're very, you know . . . funny—for a restaurant, right? It says, uh, *Colored Only*. It would be nice for the black people to get some kind of representative —not only to go around speaking and making all these speeches and all these different kind of things—I mean somebody that's going to really *show* where the black people are making progress.

I want a respectable job—clean. I was explaining it to my counselor why I wanted a job in the hospital, he came out and—bang, out of his mouth—he came out and said, "Why don't you get a job with the Sanitation Department? Why don't you be a delivery boy or something like that?" You know. I told him, I said, "Why do you think I went to school twelve years, to become a delivery boy? You must be kidding!" He said, "You want a job, right?" I said, "Well, if that's the case I don't need no job. I was doing pretty good without that before, you know." So they didn't call these couple of hospitals. He's trying to talk me out of it. He says they ain't got no opening and that their employment service at the hospital was closed at the time. They weren't hiring nobody. So I said, "Will you try another one?" So he figured, he said, "Well, that's dirty work. You going to have to be cleaning out the bedtrays and take the blood of the patients," and all this here. And I said, "Well, that's not bad. At least I'm training and eventually I won't be doing that." He said, "Then you will have to be sweeping the floor," and all this here. He called it a journeyman or something, but I said, "It's not a journeyman; it's a nurse's aide." Then he called the hospital and they told him

what it was. He said, "You were right; it was a nurse's aide." But that goes to show you how a black boy like myself tried to get a job in a white hospital with a white counselor that don't want you to get there. You see, my thing was that being I was black and he was white, he just didn't want me to get in a clean hospital or decent place to work. He wanted me to work out there in the Sanitation Department where people could laugh at me, you know, and say, well, "He's a Sanitation man, he's got to sweep the streets. He got a high school education and he's sweeping the streets. He's just a fool"—you know, like that.

I'm concerned about respect, that's what I'm concerned about. And I'm concerned about a job with respect and salary. At least I could say twelve years amounted to something. It didn't amount to $1.50 an hour, 'cause that's like saying I went to school when I could have been out in the streets shooting dice or something. I mean I make more than $1.50 shooting dice.

Well, what I'm planning to do is go and get a job at the Chase Manhattan Bank, something like that. Also I think I will go on and take the test to be a cop or something. Like if I don't really turn out myself some way I won't get no place. I'm not going to lower my pride to be no type of porter. And I'll always be like that. Long as I live. I rather starve than be somebody's porter. Just like they said, when you take a man's pride, Jim, you might rather take the man, too. Never be nobody's porter. Even if the job was a hundred fifty dollars. I'm not going to be nobody's porter. That's square business. What is pride, man? But it's the man itself, Jim. And that's me. I don't do no porter work for nobody. Don't even clean

up for myself, most like for somebody else.

Maybe I would take seventy-five dollars at like a training program at the bank 'cause I would take it and see if I could move out into another field. I get in there and get some accounting or something under my belt. Then I'll apply for junior accountancy. I got some brains. I need a good reference. I'll tell you one thing, I'm going to go to the Chase Manhattan Bank and fill out an application for a job. Then I hope I'll be able to start on Tuesday. If nothing happens I'll go down to the New York City Youth Board and see what's happening there . . .

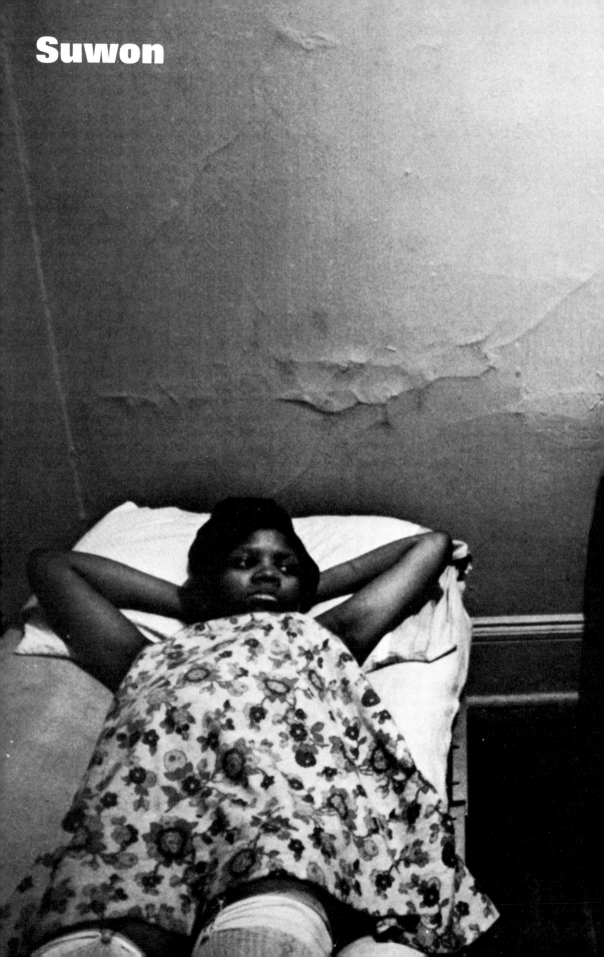
Suwon

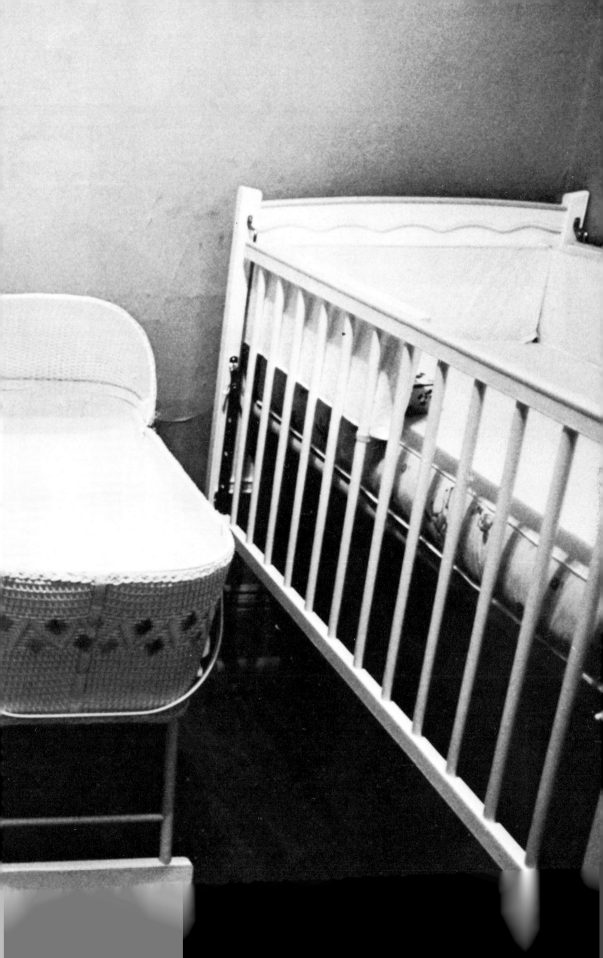

■ Suwon

When I was born I went to live with Thelma and Corwin who live in the Bronx —next to where the old Polo Grounds used to be? Near those projects over there? That's where they lived and that's where we lived as soon as I was born. My parents were there, also. We were all living in the same apartment. Then after that, me and my brother went to live with my aunt at 112th Street. My mother and father lived on 117th Street. We split then, 'cause he couldn't—he wouldn't—work, you know, to get an apartment for his wife and two kids. I don't know what it was, but we wasn't together . . . oh, for a good while. Then we went down South and was separated from my mother and father. Almost five or six years. Oh, I mean we had them, they came and saw us, but we were being raised by another aunt. After that we went to Lake City, South Carolina, with my grandmother for two years. And then . . . then my father came down there to get us and we bought the home out in Long Island. Yeah, we had a house in Central Islip on Elm Street. Uh-huh. Private house. It was beautiful.

You see, while we was down South I guess he was saving his money for us to come back up here and get the home. We lived out there for about a year. Father got this house and this is when my mother first started drinking. My father would give her money to put in the bank and pay the mortgage and she would drink it up, you see, and then my father found out and he got upset. He said, "Well, I thought that we would be finished paying for the house in three years, and we had a good nest egg in the bank and you drink it up. Red," he said, "what's wrong?" Then she started drinking more.

So he left, and then right after he left they cut our lights out, they cut the heat off, and no water. You have to pay for your water out there. There was no water. Then they cut all this off—the water, the heat and the lights. And my mother was staying there as long as she could, still drinking, staying as long as she could. Then they came and put us out, you know. They had to. So I had a aunt that lived out there in a two-story house, still in Central Islip. And we went and we lived with her. You know, my father wasn't with us now. This is the first time he left. After that we came up here, you know, in the city, to the Bronx to my Aunt Helen's house. Me and Gregory lived there, that's my brother, and my mother went and lived with my aunt on 125th Street. Now we was separated again for a year. Then my father came back and my mother took him back. So me and my brother was still living at my aunt's house in the Bronx, and my father and my mother was living with my aunt on 125th Street. My mother and my uncle had a argument, so me and my brother had to leave. So we went to my aunt at 125th Street and my mother and my father moved out to this room on 119th Street. Then my father got us this apartment on 129th Street between Lenox and Fifth. And we lived there. For two years. Then we moved to 174th Street, to this four-room apartment, where I met John.

One night I was standing in front of the Third Avenue El—you know, where you come down the stairs? And we were standing there and he started playing with me, you know; that's when I really started liking him. It was really the first time we ever had anything to say to each other. It was on a Sunday night. On the other side of the street in front of that

Spanish candy store. And he started playing with me and saying, "This is going to be my girlfriend." You know, that's how they play around there. So, anyway, after that passed and everything I'd go up to Geneva's house, to say I was going to see Geneva but really just to see John. You know, we never said anything to each other but one day we was sitting in his house and he started asking my name and everything. Then there was a Friday night, April 19th, he asked to go with me. At first I told him I didn't know. He said, "I want you for my woman." That's how he came out and said it. So I said, well, "I don't know." You know? So he said, "How long would it take for you to make up your mind?" So I said, "Well, I don't know." By the way, this was in the hallway. You know, Bull's, the candy store on Bathgate near the poolroom? Well, anyway, it was in the building next door to that. So then he left the house.

He must have prompted his sister, Geneva. We used to be good friends before I met John. He prompted her to talk to me. Anyway, she came over and she say, "Well, Suwon, John likes you a lot and he wants you to be his woman, you know, blah blah blah, and he acts wild." So they talked to me, so then we had went up to Geneva's house 'cause her mother had went out. So we were sitting in the living room. So he said what's my answer. I liked him, but you know a girl don't want to look too anxious, you know, soon as he ask her to say yes, so I said, well, I'd think about it, you know.

Now, you know, it's funny the way our relationship started. It didn't start like boyfriend or girlfriend. It's almost like sister and brother. We used to do our homework together. That's all. He used

to come up—you know how boyfriends and girls will go out and, say, neck and all this—me and John didn't do that. Only time me and John really saw each other was like after he got out of school or after I got out of school he'd come up to my house to do his homework. That is all there was. And he used to take me, or he was going to take me, to his school track things, and the prom came up. That's how we really got into it, was with the prom, cause then we started interesting in each other's school.

I was so excited about the prom, I had my gown made. A girlfriend of mine on 112th Street that lives next door to my aunt, for the making she charged—just for her work—seventeen dollars and we had to buy the material. That was my first gown . . . my first gown. And I was so excited about that. Really, yes, I was. That was my first major event . . . really . . . in my life. That was the first time I was really happy, happy, happy. You know, happy and having things work out.

You know, we were the only colored couple there? It really didn't bother me. It was just that I didn't have anybody to talk to, and John would get up and leave . . . all his friends were there. It's not just because they weren't colored, just because I didn't have anybody to say, "How you been doing, and like I saw so-and-so yesterday." General gossip. I guess being the only colored couple at that thing did bother me in a way. It didn't bother John 'cause he went to the school, and he knew . . . he saw these kids every day, day in and day out, so it wouldn't really bother him.

I was kind of depressed anyway. Like, when we went to the prom, I was sup- posed to have get my period and I didn't get it. You know, but I had been pregnant already, and then when I didn't get it for two months I said, "Well, John, something's wrong . . ." I said, "This never happen to me before." I told John, and he didn't believe it. He told me I couldn't be pregnant. I don't know. He told me I couldn't be pregnant. No explanation. I just cried. I cried. I cry because he said that he couldn't see how I was pregnant. If I was pregnant then it was his. But he was just saying he don't see how I could be pregnant. Period. I didn't go to the doctor till I was three months pregnant. He just said . . . he asked to marry me, and that he wanted to take care of it. I said that I would marry him, but I had to wait until I finished school. It didn't bother me if any of my friends found out that I was pregnant. No. 'Cause most of my friends are pregnant already, you see, so it doesn't make a difference. I was really more scared than I was, like, ashamed. You know what I'm trying to say? Like I was really more scared and I stayed awake plenty of nights just planning on how I would tell them—tell my mother and father that I was pregnant and I couldn't go to school.

I didn't really want a baby. No. Uh-uh. That was the furthest thing from my mind. No. Uh-uh. One reason I was so . . . I was so scared to even get pregnant, you know, 'cause I didn't know what my father or my mother would have done. So I didn't really want one.

In the meantime, my mother found out through people in the street. I started puffing out, I started bulging out of my clothes and, you know, in the summer I used to wear shapely clothes. So anyway, the super was very close to our family and she told my mother, she said, "Well, I think Suwon is pregnant." So my mother got me and John up in the house

and she say, she was drunk, and she said, "Are you pregnant, Suwon?" So I said, "Mama, don't start that." I say, "No, I'm not pregnant." So I got up and I left the house 'cause I knew what was coming. She was going to nag, nag, nag and it would turn into a argument. John just sat there. So, anyway. I was leaning on the corner when he came downstairs, and he told me that he had told her that I was pregnant. But what I was going to do, I was going to try to go to school three months, and after I'd got in school I was going to call my father up and ask if me and John could come to his house to sit down and talk to him, and explain to him calmly, you know. And I say, well, since I'm in school, maybe he won't take it so hard. If he see I'm trying to stay in school. Anyway, John, he couldn't hold it right there. He had to tell my mother, so my mother called my father. My father came and told me and John that we couldn't get married. He say because he want me to finish school. He just say he want me to finish school.

I don't know, but my father thought John to be very low. He said he thought John was different from the other boys out in the street. You know how some boys try to take advantage of a girl? They would have sex relations with me without any protection, and see me get pregnant. That was the opinion he had of John after he found out that I was pregnant. But as time went on he start liking John as much as he did before I got pregnant. I guess he thought it couldn't have been avoided. I guess he sat down and said, well, he was young once himself, and he know how it is with a young couple, you know, and he knows how my mother was, alcoholic and everything, that if me and John wanted to do anything

164

we were free to do it. So I guess he say he couldn't really blame John if it was right there for him. He's not going to, you know, pass it by. So. But that's the way my father thinks, you see. Because my father does it himself. That's the way he thinks. And I guess after he woke up and realized that John . . . that I had to . . . that, you know, John didn't rape me. So I guess if he wake up and realize that, he say why should I be mad. And he saw I wasn't going to give John up. So John and my father had arguments. Because John wanted to marry me. My father was going to send me down South, but John said, you know, he didn't think it was right. I was his woman, and I was pregnant for him and he didn't want me to have his child down South. So then Daddy said, "Well, I don't think you have anything to say about it." So John say, "Why shouldn't I have anything to say about it?" He say, " 'Cause if it wasn't for me she wouldn't be in this situation, you know, that she is in now." So they start arguing. He said, "I don't care what you say, she going down South." They just argue back and forth like that.

I never felt guilty. I felt scared, 'cause I didn't know what my parents was going to do. But since it had happened as it did, I was glad, but if I could have avoided it happening like that I would have tried. But since it did happen, then I was looking forward to having it.

I am looking forward with great joy. More than I did before. It just seems like . . . it seems days are so long . . . it seems like I won't get a pain until I can get this labor and get it over with. I don't know . . . seems like it's taking a long time. This month is just dragging by. The first few months went fast, 'cause I didn't find out I was definitely pregnant until I was

three months pregnant, you see, and that time it just went fast. Then when we got in after Christmas, January, and everything just slow . . . slow . . . slow . . . down.

John's changed. I don't know . . . but he has changed. He really has changed. I don't know what it is. He's more quicker to jump—mad, you know—even at my mother. And he used to respect my mother to the heights. Maybe it's her fault. But he doesn't, you know, respect her as much as he did before. Maybe that's what it is. Because she drinks and is an alcoholic. That's one of the reasons he don't have as much respect for her as he used to.

When John first met me mother wasn't drinking. Uh-uh. She never drink wine, nothing like that. She was drinking, but not an everyday thing. And you see, my father was still with us then. Then, what really started mother drinking was after my father left us. In May. Then after he left, I guess she saw that he was gone and another woman had him, and she just started getting the bottle. My mother wouldn't work. She was working but she wouldn't work. You know what I'm trying to say? Listen . . . my mother would go on these benders—she would drink. She would get a job and one day she would stay off and drink and lose the job. And the bills was piling up on my father, you know, and it got on his nerves so much, so he just had to leave and get out, that's all. Well, really why he left was because, one night she went on this bender and she had told him to get out, that she could take care of the rent and everything, so he said, "Well, Ethel, I'll tell you this, I'll pay up the rent and the light and gas bill," and he say, "then I'll leave." And he pay up the rent and light and gas bill, and left.

165

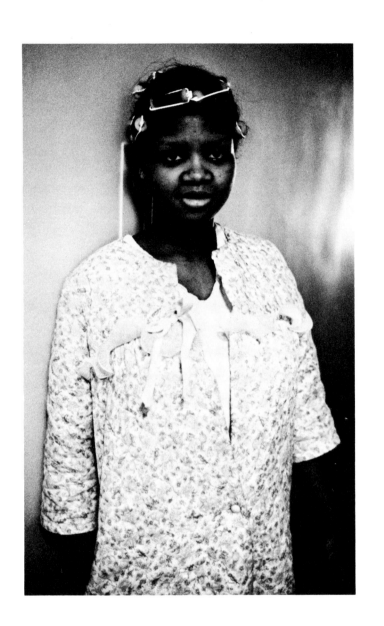

And I guess it shocked her, you know, so much she just started going to the bottle. That's when she applied for welfare. We didn't get on welfare until June really.

When my mother found out I was pregnant her feelings were, well, kind of mixed, 'cause she loved John. She loved John from the beginning, and all she had to say was since it did happen she's glad it happen by a boy like John that had the decency to ask me to marry him, you know. And since it's been such a long time since she even had a grandchild, she was glad just because she would be the grandmother. That's all. She never was against me throughout the whole thing.

My father. He's selfish, you see. And like he told everybody in the family that I'm his only girl, and he don't want to lose me this soon, you know. But he don't know. He's just losing me faster. You know, my love for him. He's losing me faster than if he would let me marry John. It's not that I would marry John—because I wasn't going to marry him anyways because . . . But if I did want to change my mind I couldn't marry him anyway. If we were to get married my mother would have to sign. Mother or father. But since my mother was on our side she was ready to sign. The papers. But he told my mother that if she would sign the papers for me to marry John then he would kill her. So to keep my mother . . . I mean I don't know if he'll kill her . . . to keep her life out of jeopardy, I just said I would wait, that's all. And when I get eighteen he can't do anything to me 'cause John will be twenty-one. So.

I still don't think John did realize that I was pregnant, you know. That's the way he went around. I mean when a boy find

out that his girlfriend is pregnant he goes out and he start looking for a job to take care of what is his, but the only time John really realize that he has a child is when he'd be seeing it. 'Cause like he said one day, he said, "You know, the child might die. All this making plans, you know . . ." He said the child just might die. It was like a everyday thing. But you see what I said what is going to happen when he does see it. It's going to shake him so much that he's going to be running like a chicken with his head cut off, trying to do the things he should have been doing five months ago. You see. That's why. He's not a very mature person. 'Cause with a mature person, you see that your girlfriend is pregnant. Even if she don't have it you'd still have the money you know that you would spend on the child. If John had money enough to start off in an apartment with me and the baby without any of my help I would marry John, I would try to marry John and go to school, too. My mother could still take care of the baby. You see, I always have my mother.

I want to go back to school and to work, right? But it wouldn't be fair to leave my mother with all that work. You see, it wouldn't be fair to my mother 'cause when I'm not there, my mother, she's going to have to wash those diapers and sterilize those bottles and all that other extra work I was bringing on myself and really on my mother, too.

My plans are delayed. Yeah. Just for the meantime, I just delayed my plans. I eventually want to be a professional secretary. I don't really know why I want to be a secretary. I guess it's just that I love to write and I love to type, and I like for things to tease my mind, you know, and a secretarial—with a nursing job it's obvious, you know, like if a patient is bleeding, stop him from bleeding—secretarial job you have to think. In a nursing job—and I can't stand the sight of blood! That's another! And I can't stand dead bodies. It seems like with secretarial, you know, it just, I like things to tease my mind, that's why . . . puzzles, and I like to think . . . so that's why I feel it'd be the best thing for me to do. And to teach . . . I just couldn't be a teacher.

But after baby grows a little I'm going to my school, which is Roosevelt, you know, High School, and I'm going to explain to them what happened, you know, just explain to them that I got pregnant, and if I could come back to the school next September, that's all. By the time I get back in school the baby'll be eight months old. You see, with a eight-months-old baby you don't have to do that much as you do with an infant, like during the summer I'll be home in the evening and at night, but during the day I'll just be working.

Geneva and I talked about getting our own apartment. You see, what had stopped that was that—I don't know—Geneva, you know, she has two kids of her own, then I have a baby, then she has to work all day and then she going to school at night, and I'm going to be going to school all day and working at night, so who's going to take care of the kids, you know? I wouldn't be really making that much money on a evening job to pay half rent, buy half food and pay for a baby-sitter. So, you know, I thought it just be more safer to stay at my mother's where I know me and my baby get taken care of until we can do better. And that's really the most important thing with a child—to have a roof over your head and somewhere to sleep. He's going to get that.

I have to give him more motherly love, and make sure he has the things that's good for him. You know, like these people out here say, well, like, "I'm going to stick my child on my mother." But my child will be at least three years old before he get out from my mother's house. That's three. Now, from three years old until he gets out on his own he will have the training he's suppose to have. 'Cause, well, how should I know, but I've gone through so much, I know right from wrong, and I know the way I came up. Oh, I don't want it to be that way for any child to come up, from one hand to another, you know, and then expect your child to respect you, when you have to go from one hand to another.

I've lost respect for my father because what he allowed happen. I lost respect for my mother because she let my father tear her down. You see, and let her get to the way she is now. You know, the alcoholic stage. That's the only reason I've lost respect for my mother. I'm not saying I don't have any respect for my father. I'm saying I lost some respect for him because he wasn't a man. Not taking care of his wife and kids, you see? I just thought, well, I said, Daddy could do better. He just didn't . . . sometimes I say maybe he can't do better because he can't find a job, but he could have done better. 'Cause he could have got any kind of job if it was just two rooms—for him and his two kids. If it was just two rooms and we had to sleep in the same bed, at least we were together. That's right. At least we were there together. That's why I say that when John thinks about these terraces, you know, these buildings with the terrace, and if he can't have that he don't want anything. As long as I have some place for me to sleep and eat—

169

and stretch out and everything—that's all that matters. And a little love, that's all.

The best treatment we ever got was when we went down South to my grand- mother. That's right. Because she had money to give us, and she didn't have anybody but her. She had the money. She had like the proper things for us . . . and I guess, one would say, the love and attention because she was lonely. She had her own home and she was there by herself and me and Greggy came and just fulfilled her life. She just loved us like a mother and a father would. That's just how it was. I have a great love and respect for her, because she had two boys and they never went out in the street cold. Her husband left her when they were babies. That's right. And they always had everything they want . . . love and every- thing else.

You know, I feel I've matured a lot in the last few months. I mean, why should you remain a kid, when you bringing one in the world? You see? So I just thought, "Suwon, it's time for you to think about what you was thinking about when you was seven and eight years old, your plans, put them into practice right now. You know, put them into operation right now. Your plans that you had when you was a little girl. Now is the time for you to start making them work. With or with- out John. About being a secretary or finishing school or having my own apart- ment . . . things like that." And having a little baby . . . a little child to love. I used to sit in the dark and cry and say, "Oh, God, just let me get grown." So I can get out of all this confusion and, you know, all this mess, and it happened for me, but in the wrong way. You know. I had to get pregnant for it to really happen.

I had a cousin and I love her from the day she use to say—I use to go in the room and cry—and she say, "Don't cry, Suwon, when we grow up we going to finish school and I'm going to be a doctor and you going to be a secretary and like we would get this apartment. And we have boyfriends, and we have children and we move away and have these homes." 'Cause, you see, my aunt had willed her home to me. This two-story house, but then she and her husband had broken up. So that just, you know, I just got left out. Me and my cousin used to talk about moving into that house, me and her, and her husband and my hus- band. Moving in this two-story house, and living together and having the kids go out in the backyard and play together, you know how you used see the pictures on the television.

You can live in the worst neighborhood long as you have a good home. You don't have to go out in the street. Long as you have a good home to live in. 174th Street. It's a hard neighborhood to get along with, you know. It just seem like it's so rough and really dangerous to walk down the street. Like, if you a stranger and you come in the block, they'll take you off in a minute. But if they know you and you live in the block, how could you have more than they got. You know. White. Black. I don't care which one. Anytime of day. It seems like the block, well, the neighborhood is a little city. It seems like. I don't know. It just seem like it's a little city. When you go out of it you could tell when you're out of it, and when you get in you get this feel of it. Like a little Peyton Place, really. I mean, a few blocks is your world. Like 'cause I never went out, and this is where I met John. That's how it came to me. It came just like . . . like there was no other place but this.

It's up to the people to make what they want out of themselves. See, it depends on the person what happens to them. Like I had this friend, Rosalind. We used to live on 129th Street together, then we moved in the block and she just . . . seemed like she changed . . . I don't know. She just started using dope. First she started with . . . reefers and she started with they call it snorting, snorting up dope, and now she's skin-popping, you know . . . gradually, gradually she's going further and further. It wasn't the neighborhood. The neighborhood don't really rule your mind if you let it. Now, you see, I could have become a dope addict just like . . . not really a dope addict . . . but I could have started using dope just like Rosalind. Me and Rosalind used to go everywhere together. Everywhere. We used to go shopping together, we used to go to school together. We used to go spend the night at each other's house, you know. Now if the neighborhood really ruled me I could have started using dope like Rosalind. I mean Rosalind started smoking reefers.

But Gregory, my brother, he's different from anybody else on the block. The only time one saw my brother was when he was leaving out of the block or coming in. Gregory didn't even go to the store in that block. He just didn't want part of it. You know. Me, I had to go out and see what's what, but he doesn't care. He's very smart. One sees Gregory going to school and Gregory coming back. That's it. He studies constantly. That's all he had to do. He didn't go out 'cause he didn't like the block. He went to I.S. 201 when we were living in Manhattan. He didn't even want to go to any of the schools up there. He went all the way to 127th Street. He wants to be a doctor. And

he's going to make it too, watch. My mother and brother don't get along. And my father thought it was best—since Gregory was so smart, and he needed a quiet home to study in—he decided it was best for him to go with my aunt where he could.

He's so quiet, he don't say nothing to you, you know, unless you say something to him. So I really don't know why she picks him to pick on. He's in the ninth grade, got a twelfth-grade reading level. It's a gift. He ain't never really had time to read. He looks like he's ten, he's so small, but he's almost fourteen. You see, with my brother, he says, "You got what you got. I'm not going to hurt myself to get more than I have. You know, what I got, I'm just going to do the best with what I got." Like he asked my father for a leather coat two years ago. And he didn't get it yet. He asked him once and he saw that he wasn't going to get it, so he forgot it. But with me, I asked for my suede coat a month before Christmas and I was supposed to get it Christmas. I didn't get it until two months after Christmas, but I got it. That's right. I kept on bugging and bugging, but Gregory's not like that. He ask you once, you don't give it to him, that's it. He's a very calm person, he don't get upset.

He's different from John, altogether. John, he wanted to be the big man. In the neighborhood John wanted those people to think he had more than they did, you know. Like I remember looking at wedding rings . . . well, not really wedding rings, just any kind of rings—something to show I meant something to him. It's he that wanted it. I don't . . . just as long as I know I go with you, that's all. He just had to have some kind of proof, but he don't know what to do with it. He

171

don't even want to take care of it. That's all he shows is an interest. He don't try to do, you know, what's right. I wouldn't care if I didn't see John but once a month, long as I knew he was out there trying to better himself or better, you know, conditions for his child. I don't know. If I knew he was out there doing something that was worthwhile. If he was out there trying to do something for himself or, you know, a job, if he had a job. Then I wouldn't say anything.

John just seems different than he was before, when I first met him. When I met John it was fun. And now it just seems like an everyday thing. When we used to be in the neighborhood we used to run through the streets. That was a good time. Maybe because we didn't have any problems and he could work when he got ready. All there was really to think about was school. He was so involved in his school. You know we used to do our homework together, and now it's just that he has to get a job. And it seems like everything is pressing down now. I'm beginning to feel like I'm a burden to John. He don't even run track any more. And he loves that. I'm getting a lower and lower opinion of him. And he doesn't realize it. John doesn't do what's right. He don't have to break his back to show that he's trying, you know. Even if he don't work but one week—just show that he's trying. I don't know what it is. I wish I did. I don't know what it is. If I move out of that apartment I have to move with John. Now, he's going to say, "Well, now, you moving out. If you going to move with Geneva, why can't you move out with me?" But how can you move with a person that won't even get a job? Geneva works each and every day. Now, how can you move with a person won't even

get a job? He rather me live with him and be poor. He's just lazy. He thinks that the job's supposed to come to him.

Like when my cousin got pregnant, her boyfriend worked like a dog to get them out of their house by the time she had the baby. And after she had the baby, after she came home, he had the apartment for them to get married, you know. And he had the rent paid up for two months. And I mean had furniture in the house. I mean he worked like a dog. Day and night. And you know it made her feel good.

Well, John'll get himself straightened out one of these days, and when he does I guess he'll be straightened out for life 'cause it seem like he's really looking for a job for life. And he's trying to show me that he's trying to get this job, you know. And, like at one point he was telling me he's working when I know he's not really working. Maybe it's my fault. It just that he don't want nobody else doing anything for me or the baby. You know. But it's not making me feel any better if he's lying and he don't realize that. If he would just come out and say, "Well, Suwon, I'm trying to find a job which I have a good future in." And "I don't know about this porter job, you know." Then I would say, "Well, all right. John. Take your time."

I know he's doing it for me, so that's why I don't even say anything. Every time he gets money, you know, he tries to get something for the baby. Like the other day he bought the baby some rubber pants. 'Cause he heard me complaining about the baby didn't have any rubber pants. The baby didn't have any lotion to go on it, no comb and brush, you know, not real necessities, but things I wanted for it. And so he went out and bought some rubber pants and he left them at his mother house.

He just seems more like himself then. Like I told him that night, I said, "John, you changed at one time." He said, "What do you mean?" He don't even realize that he changed. But he did. But he's changing back. His same old gay self. Like that night really, really reminded me of the times we used to have on 174th Street. It really did. You know, he's just changing back slowly. He's going right back into his track. You know what I mean and his school. I was surprised that night that he told me he sometimes lost at track. He told me about the times he lost and how he felt. That's the honest John. But if he was the John that he was beginning to change into he would have said, "Well, I never lost." You know what I mean? "I never lost. 'Cause I was the greatest, and I never lost anything." That night he just came out and told me how he felt when he did lose. You know. He told me quite a few times about how he lost and who he lost to. And everything.

I know John is trying to change to his old self. When I first met him I remember John had one pair of sneakers and some quarter-gaiters or half-gaiters or something. But they couldn't have cost more than twenty dollars. And he wore those until, I mean, they really went out. And those sneakers, he wore them every day. Every day. I couldn't say anything 'cause I knew he couldn't do any better. Then he used to come to my aunt's house, she got carpets on every inch of her floor. I mean they were really fabulous. And I guess he felt kind of funny coming in there. He wanted something to prove to them like Suwon got a good man, so he used to buy these forty-dollar shoes, these twenty-dollar shirts, these sixteen-dollar

pants, you know what I mean? Like that white leather jacket. John didn't need that white leather jacket. John could have took that money he spent on that white leather jacket and got him a long winter coat for the winter. But instead, just because I had got that gray coat—I had my suede coat, you know—I'm not trying to say that he was jealous of me, it's just that he didn't want me, you know, looking any better than he was. That's where all his money went. Instead of it being in the bank, that's where it went.

Now his mother don't have any money 'cause she's trying to pay this lawyer. He can't depend on his mother no more. So he's just changing right back. He's doing with what he got. That's the way I want him. You know, just to do with what you got.

Then last night he changed again. He said, "Suwon, I want to marry," he said, "this week. When I get paid, next week," he said, "I'm going to spend this paycheck on the baby's clothes." Then he said, "And the next paycheck I'm going to take it and put it down on my apartment, and the next paycheck I'm going to take it and I'm going to pay for my apartment." And he said, "The next paycheck I'm going to get me and I'm going to put some furniture in my house." And that was seventy-five dollars. So he said, "The next paycheck I'm going to get me a color television, from the first, so I won't have to be worrying about it later on. I want me a color television." He said, "I'm just going to get it." Then he said he was going to get all this fabulous furniture and paint his apartment. Black and orange and . . . And he was just changing right back into the same old John. Then I looked at John, I said, "Well, John, you really think you can do all

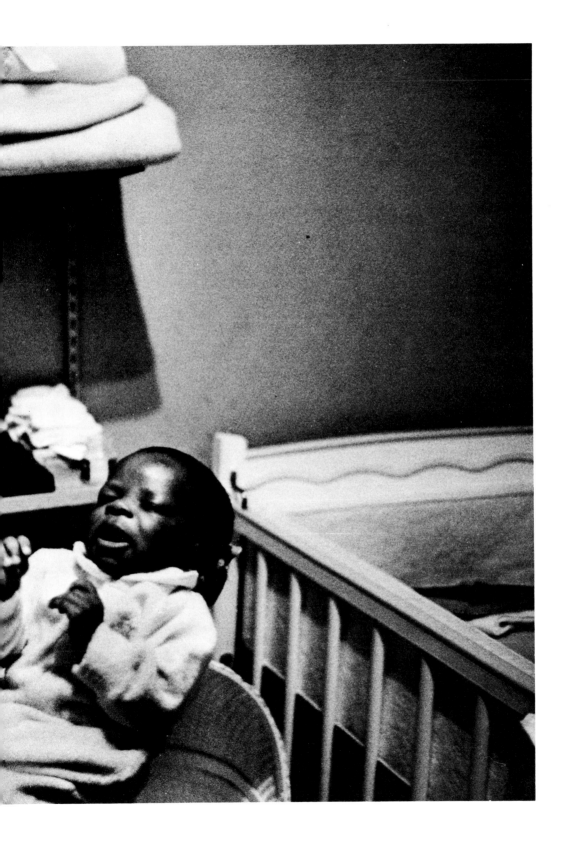

that?" Like that. He said, "Yeah." He said, "I'm going to do it." But he can't do that. Because he can't. So I just told him, well, "John, you can't do that." So he didn't say any more about it. Usually he would have argued. But he didn't say anything more.

See, it's not that I don't want John to get a job where he's not the big man, but I hope that he gets a job that pays well enough to get money soon. Instead of getting a job for seventy-five dollars a week I think it'd be smart to get a porter job working for ninety dollars a week. Especially if he wants to marry me bad. That's what I would explain to him if I could talk to him. Maybe he would listen to me if I was to tell him that.

When my father was with us I had the money to buy the clothes I wanted, shoes every week. So I guess John got it in his mind now like I want a man that's going to give me these shoes and these clothes. So I guess that's why he's tried to really impress me. Only he don't know. I don't want him to do something like scrubbing floors all his life. If he could do what he really wants to do I think it's a good thing. Like he said he wanted a job with a future. So sometime in the future he can do what he enjoys instead of getting up in the morning and saying, "Well, I'm going to have to scrub the floors and put the lights up in the hallway all my life." That really discourages a person—to go and do this day in and day out all your life. Maybe that's why he don't want to take it, 'cause maybe that's what he think —that white people just trying to trick him into doing this a year, then when the year is up then say, well, you have to do it another half a year, then another year and another year. He wants an office job, a bank job or something like that. He

wants to be a teller or an accountant or something like that. Maybe if he saw a white boy being a porter, being an attendance man . . . doing it, you know, maybe he would feel better. But he thinks that the white men take the black people as their underdogs. Like, "You do this, and I'll be up in my office and while I'm up in my office I know where all the black people are. Cleaning the floors and making sure the building is clean."

All I want him to do is try it. If he don't like it, then all I can say is, well, at least he did try. That he do want to get me out of here, but if he's just going to stand up and say no, without even trying, I say, "Well, he don't really want to marry me." If he's going to pass up an opportunity like that. I don't want no man that's going to go right up on the top and he can fall down. I want somebody that's going to work hard and when he gets to the top he's going to stay there. And I don't want none of these fast job. That's what John likes. Something that's real fast and he thinks he can get it even if it's twenty-five cents a week. That's the way he wants it. I really do love John, and he doesn't realize it. He says that I'm going to jive him. Does that make any sense? Messing around with somebody else? I said, "Well, John, you know, what do you want me to do to prove to you I want you?" He say, "Time will tell." So I guess I'm on trial. But we really did have fun the other night. Because he has his track jacket from high school and we was talking about track and everything. And he was telling me how he started off. And how you run and you have to kneel down. He was showing me that. And one of his friends died in Vietnam, and he was showing me his picture and telling me about the good times they had together.

We really had fun laughing and we didn't get to sleep till about four or five in the morning. And I had wonderful dreams.

I used to dream about the baby a lot and the eyes was so big, look like his eyes was his whole face. His eyes was big and was real, real light. Real light. Had straight hair and was kind of skinny, though. Kind of small. I don't know if it was a boy or a girl. 'Cause like with the first few days I didn't see it with any clothes on, so I couldn't tell if it was a boy or a girl. John asked me the same thing. When I'd talk about my dreams, he said, "What was it, a boy or a girl?" And I said, "I couldn't tell you." At first I wanted a girl. And then I wanted a boy, but the only reason I wanted a boy was that I thought a boy would be cheaper to dress but since everybody says it just as much difference, I didn't care what it is as long as it's healthy. That's all.

John said he wanted a boy because it was his first. I said, "Well, it doesn't seem right for him to have a girl." Not as his first. Even if this is the only boy I have, and I have all girls after . . . just as long as I have this boy. In a way it seemed like he deserves a boy. He's such a track star, how would it look teaching a girl track and football and basketball? I really wanted a boy. Before it really didn't matter to me long as it was a baby. It didn't really matter if it was a girl or a boy. If it'd be a girl, well, I can't do any-thing, anyway. 'Cause to me, I could want a girl too, because I could dress her and get its ears pierced. But for John's sake, 'cause it doesn't make a dif-ference to me, but it makes a difference to him. So, if he wanted a boy I wanted a boy, too.

I was fixing up the room to prepare for the baby 'cause I was getting very anxious. 'Cause when I first got the crib and bassinet from John, I was saying, "Well, you know, I've got the crib and bassinet; all I need is the baby." And I started getting worried about when the baby was going to come. You see, the crib and bassinet just made me more anxious. I wanted to have the baby then, when I got the crib and bassinet. I wanted the baby. That just the way it made me feel. I used to wish the crib was filled with the baby already. And I said, "Then when it gets here I'll start worrying about the problems. I know it's got to come. I don't know how it's coming, but it'd have to come."

'Cept I used to worry about the mice. One night me and John was sitting here and a little mice crawled through the door and it must have hurt itself 'cause it was screaming and screeching. I was so em-barrassed because John was here. I said, "Oh, God," and it was in my . . . room, you know. And I know the baby's going to have to be here and I can't just sit here, you know, and watch the mice. That's why I said I need a trap in here in case they do come anywhere around the crib or bassinet. I don't want it no-where next to the baby. Everybody says, "Well, it don't bite." It bit that candy I left on the TV, and if it bit that candy it'll try to bite my baby. And that candy is much harder than the skin on my baby.

I'm not just going to take my child in any kind of neighborhood. I'll try to find the best for him 'cause I don't want my child growing up like everybody else in the neighborhood. If he has the right bringing up he won't. My parents didn't do a good job taking care of us, like shoving us from one house to another, but at least we are all here today. I'm fifteen and my

brother is fourteen. So fifteen or sixteen years from now we'll be here. Me and John. And we'll teach our children to just get out and get your own. Don't depend on anybody else. Just get out on your own. Learn to be independent. Don't have to listen to nobody. And like if you get married, help your husband or your wife out. I mean you don't have to bow down to them and say, well, "Kiss my behind, because I do this for you and I do that." Teamwork is the best work in the world. That's all. Love to me is just trusting a person.

Nine whole months. Seemed like twenty. To just wake up and see that it's there . . . you say, well, what happen? I just told Mom that I had a pain. She said, "Well, let's get ready and let's go." She started taking the curlers out of my hair and telling me to get ready. See, I was still sitting there without my coat, without my suitcase, without anything. Then Mama and Gregory was going out the door looking for John to get a cab. So, finally they found John playing pool around the corner. I said, "Well, I'll just go." And so I went. This was about five o'clock. I didn't think I was going to stay, and I hated to come to the hospital like a fool, making a fool out of myself and telling them my contractions were ten minutes apart.

When we got in there and I went up in the labor room and they started pricking me and everything and did all the routine things. Then at one-thirty the pains was coming real hard, so I asked the doctor for a painkiller. So he gave me a painkiller in my vagina. That's all I had. That painkiller. Three hours later I felt like I had to . . . not urinate . . . I had to move my bowels. I told them to bring me a

bedpan 'cause I have to go to the bathroom. So this nurse, this nasty nurse, she came in, she just swished in, and she said, "I'm telling you if you're not finished with this bedpan I'm not bringing this bedpan in here every ten minutes. Because if you have to do anything you'd better do it, and if you crap in that bed you're going to lay in it." I said, "Miss, listen, I can feel it. I'm finished." "Oh, I'm telling you," she said, "if you crap in that bed, you're going to lay in it." And I couldn't. When my water broke a little bit I got up out of bed and told her to change that bed. Not her, the nurse that was in there with me. Because I couldn't bear them pains and be in that bed—all sticky and slimy.

I was in a room by myself; I wasn't on a ward. They put me in a private room. I was praying to have somebody. I didn't care who it was. Just to hold my hand. Just do something. And I thought sure they were going to let Mom in. Why wouldn't they let Mommie up there. Why wouldn't they let Mom up there? When Momma first took me to the nurse in the Emergency Room they said that she couldn't come, that she would hear from me or could go up and see me within an hour to see if I was staying awake. Mommie never came back. I just wanted her there . . . I wanted her there. I can't stand to have pain around John 'cause he treats me so much like a baby. I can't stand for nobody to treat me like a baby. Every time I caught a pain in the taxi coming to the hospital, he'd open my coat, shut my window . . . he was being affectionate. I guess he was. But at least with my mother, I get a pain, she says, "All right, Suwon, it'll be over soon." John don't tell you that; he tries to pat your head.

But I felt love for John. I don't measure

it, but he was on my mind. I said, "John, I don't care how long it takes," and I kept on looking at that clock. But when I was laying there, five minutes wasn't going too fast. Five minutes felt like an hour. Yeah, seemed like I fell in love with John all over again. I said, "John, I'm going to have your baby. I don't care what happens." I said, "I'm going to have it. I'm having this pain, but I'm going to have it."

I kept on getting up out of the bed 'cause the pain hit me so hard I couldn't lay down, I couldn't be on my side— they hit me so hard, you know. I sat up on the side of the bed with my feet hanging on the floor, so the nurse'd say, "Please get back in bed." I said, "I can't get back in that bed. These pains hit me too hard." So she went out of the room, and while she went out I really tried. The contractions had stopped for a minute. So I laid down. And she thought she was slick. She came and put the bars up on the bed. And those contractions would come and I said, "Nurse, put them bars off there. I'm going to jump over them bars." I swear I wanted to jump over these bars.

This is a good hospital though. They comfort you while you're in pain. I mean there's nothing they could do. And there wasn't no point in giving me a painkiller. But they tried to comfort you, and when I was having contractions they was saying, "How much would you like your baby to weigh, and who would you like your baby to look like? Do you want a girl or a boy?" To get my mind off the contractions. But that didn't help. And this one nurse, boy, I wouldn't let her touch me. I'd go into contractions and she was supposed to push the baby down but I wouldn't let her touch me.

The nurse say, "That's probably just the baby's head pushing down." I say, "Well, whatever it is it's going to come out of my behind." 'Cause it felt like it was going to come out of my behind. So every time a contraction hit, automatically I would strain—I couldn't help it. So she said, "Don't strain, don't strain." She said, "Don't strain." Then she was telling me she saw the head coming out and the doctor came talking about "It's not time yet, it's not time." So the head comes out another little ways, so she said, "Doctor, this girl is going to deliver this baby right here in this bed if you don't take her right in." So he took me into the Delivery Room, but on my way there I could feel the baby's head, you know.

I was begging the doctor to deliver it. I said, "Doctor, please, I have to go in that Delivery Room." I say, "If you don't, I want you to induce it." He said, "Do you really want me to induce your baby because of some pain?" I said, "You don't know how these pains feel." He said, "Well, you know this is the way they are and they'll be awhile longer." Yeah, just awhile longer. Because he couldn't give me another painkiller, you see. Oh, it was funny. I gave that little nurse a hard time. Every time she'd touch me I'd push her away from me. And he had to break my water bag, you know, and instead of it coming out all at one time—gushing out like it was supposed to come out—it came out like a dripping faucet. And when it came out, it really came out good; I started throwing up bile, the yellow spit, you know, that's so funny it tastes like medicine. My water was breaking down in my vagina and the nurse was trying to hold the pan up and trying to see the water that was breaking. It was funny, blood and water breaking, and vomiting at the mouth. She said, "Ohhh," and she went in the Delivery Room with me. And the doctor cut me from my rectum to my vagina. And the baby just flipped out. The pain left, everything left. I just felt like I could turn over and go to sleep.

4:53 in the morning. February 20. I was in labor almost eleven hours.

I heard it crying. That's when I started crying. You know, he didn't even tell me what it was, but when it was halfway out the midwife said, "All right, what you want?" Like that. So I said, "A boy." She said, "All right, here it comes." And he just came out, just like that. I knew I was going to have a boy. Maybe I couldn't say I knew. But I just had a strong feeling. I couldn't see nothing but a boy. I couldn't see pink. All I saw was blue. And sure enough here he is, a boy. John Smith, Jr., I named him. Seven pounds four ounces. I think I could have did better. As big as I was and only a seven-pound baby.

I felt so relieved the contractions was gone, and I was tired and I didn't go to sleep. Not one minute during my whole labor I didn't go to sleep. And I was so tired I just felt like turning over with me and my baby and going to sleep. And they let me hold the baby while they was stitching me up. Blood and everything. While they was stitching up I was holding the baby and I was crying and he was crying. The doctor said, "Look at this, we got two babies to take care of." I said, "No, I'm not . . ." Just so glad it was over.

My father, he just came and said, "You did a good job, Suie." He said, "You have a healthy little boy there." He said, "He's a cute little fellow." I said, "Thank you." When my mother came here she was happy and she said she saw her baby.

She said, "I'm going to take my baby home 'cause these people here don't feed my baby good. I'm going to take him home and feed him, and you better not say nothing." I said, "All right." She showed her happiness more than John did. But John's happiness was pride. You know what I mean? He was in the Emergency Room all night. He was proud because he was a father and he just came real coolly and he said, "I saw the baby, you know." He was telling me how strange he looks 'cause he so small and so white, you know. He said he was glad it was a boy. He was expecting it, you know.

I think he looks just like John. A lot of hair. Black slick hair. But yesterday when I was holding him and the nurse'd give him to me, he looked just like me, he looked like Mommie, he looked like John. He looked like everybody. Soon as he came out, though, I said that's John all over. When John came up after the baby was born he just asked me how I felt, that's all. He was excited. But how can you be excited when you're tired? I was so tired after the baby was born, that instead of me laughing and being gay, I cried. 'Cause that's all I could do. That's all I had the strength to do is cry.

And Daddy said, "John, you and Suwon can get married now. Suwon is happy." So John was talking something about how he was going to be a pro ballplayer or something, so Daddy said, "Well, if you be a pro ballplayer I'll pay for the wedding," or something like that. I wasn't really there. But John had told me. It was the next day or that night he told me, "Your father said I can marry you. If you would be happy." So what could I say? John knew where I stood. If I can't see John with a steady, good job and

182

some money coming in the house every week I'm not going to marry John. And he knows that. Geneva thinks that's wrong. She really does. You know Geneva really thinks you can live off love. She was so in love with Eddie, you know what I mean? But I know I can't live off love.

I am a little depressed. At the same time I'm very happy. I know he's there. At least I'm not waiting for him to come out. I don't feel as depressed as I was when I was pregnant. I thought he wasn't going to ever come, but now he's here and I know as long as I take care of him nothing's ever going to happen to him. But you see, when he was in my stomach there wasn't nothing I could do. But now. Long as he's here. I don't care if he's a hundred miles away, long as I know he's where he's supposed to be, and I know he's mine, that's all. I just fed him yesterday for the first time. I don't necessarily have to be feeding him. The nurses take care of that. Just as long as he's close to me. Long as I know he's eating. I can't stand a baby that don't eat good. 'Cause it worries me. But if they gobble up and be greedy that makes me feel better than a baby that is skinny and won't eat. And I felt sorry for him because he was circumcised today and he ain't eating. "Poor thing. It's all my fault because I wanted you circumcised." I can't wait to take him home.

■ A Child

I would like to live in a nice clean neighborhood—in a house. It's hard to describe. With about seven rooms with nice clean walls—with enough space to play in. So I'll have a playroom. I want enough room to play. One room would be pink, one would be red, one would be yellow, one would be blue, one would be white and one would be black.

Me and my family would live there and we would have enough space to play in the rooms, all of us children. I would have a basketball thing, I would have dolls for them, a sewing machine and an easy bake oven—a toy oven that you plug in and works like a real oven. We would have a backyard to play in. My mother would have a pretty rug, and she would have, what's the name again?—a vacuum cleaner. All my friends that are good I'll invite over to my house. I'll play with them.

We would have a station wagon for a car. A black station wagon. We would have some pets like some fish and some birds. And we would have a big old dresser with a mirror. We don't have a mirror now. My mother and father would sleep in the bed together instead of like now where my mother and brother and sisters sleep on the big bed and my father has to sleep on the couch in the living room by himself because there's no room on the bed. It's not right now because boys aren't supposed to sleep with girls. We don't have enough room for my brother to sleep in a room by himself. In my house I would only sleep with my sisters.

I would like to live in a nice clean world without so much garbage. It's filthy. People just throw it all around. A place where everybody's nice and don't throw garbage out the windows and throw garbage at you.

I would like a world without people shooting you because you don't have any money on you and nobody to catch you in a dark alley and shoot you. I see a lot of fights: people getting cut up—stabbed, shot . . . I would like the wars to stop. No wars. Nice clean decent people, everyday people that don't want to see nobody get hurt and don't want to be hurt. Things like that.

But I guess the house I would like to live in would be an ordinary house. The house wouldn't make no difference; it would be the neighborhood that makes the difference in the people. The people in the neighborhood that would make the difference. I would like to live around nice people and people that don't kill and people that like you and I like them.

It would be no special house. They're all the same. A house is a house as long as I had enough rooms to play and enough room to sleep in.

Why should I want a special house? As long as I had better people around me.

The neighborhood is the thing that's wrong.

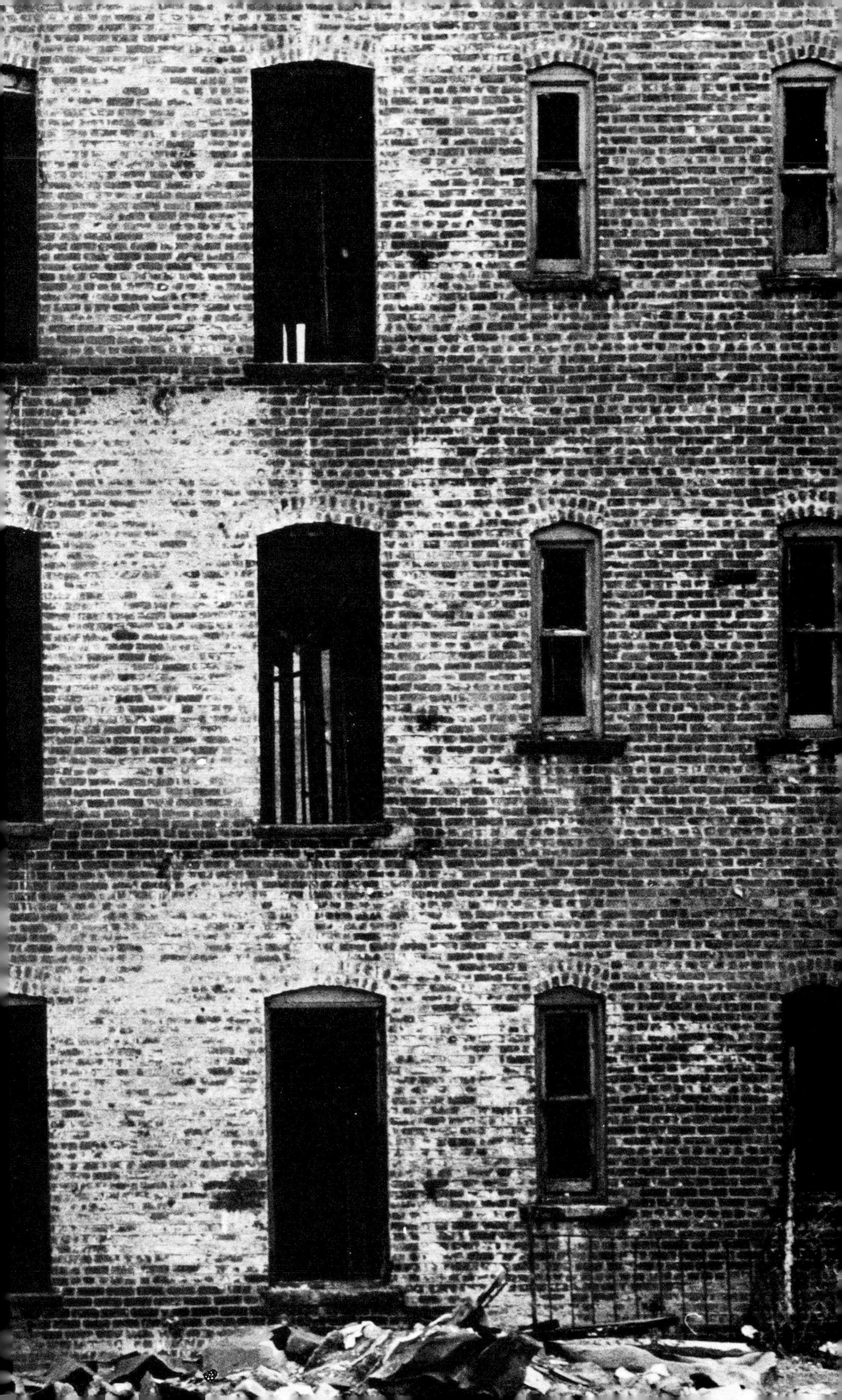

■ Notes on the Photographs

pages ii–iii: The block. The buildings in the foreground and the lot between them are the focus of the book. All the mothers and tenants interviewed, and Geneva and John Smith, live in these two buildings. This is the lot the landlord and the super's wife refer to.

page 8:   The lot.

page 9:   The super's wife.

pages 10–11:   Playing in the lot.

page 15:   A junkman making his living from refuse in the lot.

pages 16–17:   Sleeping on the fire escape on a hot day; the lot is beneath.

pages 21–22:   A child has fallen after scaling the structure of the elevated train.

page 23:   A victim of a street fight.

page 25:   Children sniffing glue; children smoking.

page 27:   A victim of a car accident under the El.

pages 30–31:   Fires in the lot.

page 36:   The bathroom of apartment 2B.

page 50:   A boy living with his grandparents, who still have nine children of their own in the apartment. This child of the oldest son was rejected by his father's second wife.

page 51:   The aunt of the boy on page 50. She is the youngest child in the family, and the only girl.

page 62:   Playing in an abandoned building.

page 63:   Playing with a fire hydrant to escape the summer heat.

page 68:   Window of a Puerto Rican storefront church.

page 75:   The family in apartment 2A: a grandmother who is raising her granddaughter.

pages 76–77:   A seventeen-year-old mother whose husband has recently abandoned her.

pages 88–89:   The man is a boyfriend who was temporarily living in the apartment.

pages 98–99:   Geneva and her first child.

pages 102–103:   Geneva awaiting the birth of her second child.

page 108:   James.

■ About the Author

HERB GORO is a professional photographer whose work was awarded certificates of merit by the Art Directors Club of New York in 1966, and by the Art Directors Club of Washington, D.C., in 1968. His photographs have appeared in various national and international publications, including *New York Magazine, Look* and *Popular Photography.*

Mr. Goro was graduated from the City College of New York. He has been both a teacher and a social worker in New York City. He now lives in Brooklyn with his wife and one-year-old daughter.

LIBRARY
College of St. Scholastica
Duluth, Minnesota 55811